NECESSARY ILLUSION

NECESSARY ILLUSION

ART AS WITNESS

Gilbert J. Rose, M.D.

INTERNATIONAL UNIVERSITIES PRESS, INC.

Madison   **Connecticut**

INTERNATIONAL UNIVERSITIES PRESS and IUP (& design) ® are registered trademarks of International Universities Press, Inc.

Library of Congress Cataloging-in-Publication Data

Rose, Gilbert J., 1923–
    Necessary Illusion : art as witness / Gilbert J. Rose
        p.   cm.
    Includes bibliographical references and index.
    ISBN 0-8236-3510-4
    1. Art—Psychological aspects.   2. Artists—Psychology.
    I. Title.
    N71.R677   1996
    701'.15—dc20   95-8950
                                                                                    CIP

Manufactured in the United States of America

To
IRMA
from music
with love

ACKNOWLEDGEMENTS

As this work unfolded, the attunement and resonance of friends and colleagues—their faith and feedback—represented responsive and reasonable "witnessing" at its best.
May others be as fortunate as I in these:

Martian Azarian and Margaret Emery
Maria V. and Martin S. Bergmann
Sidney J. Blatt
Stuart Feder
Eugene L. Goldberg
Lucy Daniels Inman
Deirdre O'Donohue
Lisa Reese
Morton F. Reiser

CONTENTS

Self-consciousness . . . exists only by being acknowledged.
—Hegel (1807, p. 111)

Only when the object exists does desire exist, only when desire exists does the object exist; desire and its object are twins, neither of which is born a fraction of an instant before the other.
—Kierkegaard (1843, p. 78)

We have no knowledge of what we feel; we have to see it in others in order to recognize it. What we recognize becomes real only after we have experienced it beforehand. It first lies within, without our being able to name it; and then, all of a sudden, there it is, as a work of art, and what happens to others becomes a memory within: at this moment it becomes real.
—Elias Canetti

INTRODUCTION:
TOWARD A PSYCHOLOGY
OF ART AND AFFECT

Essentially, this book is the last of a trilogy addressed largely to a particular concern. Just as the discovery and exploration of the "psychopathology of everyday life" has necessarily short-changed its silent creativity, the traditional clinical-psychoanalytic "take" on art, pathologizing it, does likewise to major creativity. The presumption persists that art mirrors a struggle with illness, if more or less self-healing.

There is merit to the criticism, coming largely from outside psychoanalysis that, however true this may be, it obscures as much as illuminates; and is ultimately reductive in that it does not return us to the work of art with added appreciation of what makes it creative rather than just a piece of work.

My approach redresses this focus. It studies aesthetic *form* primarily rather than *content*. In addition, it views aesthetic sublimation as evolving within a theory of reality and perception more than motivation and defense.

It assumes that any work reflects its author's ego doing what any healthy ego does in its everyday performance:

selecting from a full repertoire of functions to adapt to a present task in the light of past experience. Thus, there will be elements that are defensive and adaptive, regressive and progressive, private and communicative. It assumes, too, that the formal dynamic structure of art mirrors and magnifies mind in action. Hence, art can be a tactic for exploring psyche.

Accordingly, *The Power of Form* (1980) focused on the correspondence between aesthetic form and psychic process, construing each as involving an interplay between two different ways of organizing data: wide focus, holistic imagination and sharp focus, realistic thought and perception. This highlighted the adaptive role of art—like ego—in helping to orient one in terms of time, space, and identity in an inconstant reality.

The notion of homologous structures between art and mind turned out to be a *re*discovery for myself of Arnheim's (1949) fruitful idea of isomorphism. It drew me to the idea that the interaction between art and mind—based on their corresponding structures—may be viewed as a form of *resonance* (Webster: *music*—supplementary vibration sympathetically induced). Next, that this either generates or is associated with currents of affect (*Trauma and Mastery in Life and Art*, 1987).

Art stands on its own—an essentially autonomous balance of forces. It also exists in a dynamic relationship to the response of its audience. Exploring the emotional resonances to art with one eye on contemporary affect theory and the other on a nonreductionist psychology of art is our present enterprise.

In the discussion to follow, little effort will be made to distinguish feelings as awareness of affect, affect as including the bodily changes that accompany it with or without awareness, and emotion as a complex mixture including personal memories and associations.

1

A "WITNESSING" PRESENCE

From time immemorial, creative art evokes latent emotions that permit new meanings to become manifest; in this century, psychoanalysis has also done this. Art provides highly refined sensorimotor nutriment; psychoanalysis, a unique form of reflective discourse. Each may be viewed as a "witnessing" presence, the subjective essence of which involves an experience of empathic interaction; with this, comes emotion.

The idea of a "witnessing" presence is a way of indicating two things: a participating recipient is provided with the wherewithal—sensorimotor or verbal discourse—to create an experience of a holding, responsive presence; within such a protective framework, one has the opportunity and "permission" to stop and hear, see, experience—with feeling—what was always present in oneself in some form or other but, to a greater or lesser extent, inaccessible.

Psychoanalysis and art do not stand alone as forms of empathic interaction that serve to bear witness to latent aspects of oneself accompanied by a flow of emotion. Nor does adding love and friendship in their myriad forms exhaust the range of possibilities. Let us begin by sketching some

1

examples in order to establish this working context and indicate something of its wide range.

Prompters

After a swim at the local Y, I unexpectedly ran into an old friend. We entered the sauna together: "So, how are you?" "Terrible!" he groaned, and went on to regale me with a litany of complaints about his life, his marriage, his work. As a professional actor of some renown he had enjoyed considerable success. But *enjoy* maybe is the wrong word. He complained bitterly about his many years in the theater, speaking into that black hole beyond the footlights. For what? It's all an illusion. Empty. To say nothing of his marriage. No secret to his friends. Finally, bucking up a little: "You're coming to the theater this evening, aren't you?" he said. "You know you can always count on me," I grunted as I left the sauna irritable by then and kind of depressed. "And to the party afterwards," he called, still more airily.

It turned out to be a one-act play by Chekhov, *The Swan Song*, with my friend in the lead role of Svietlovidoff, a comedian, 68. The scene is the stage of a country theater, at night, after a play.

> *Svietlovidoff*: I fell asleep in my dressing room when the play was over. [Calls his servants] Not a sound! Only echoes answer me. The rascals have gone off and have probably locked up the theatre. It's no use! I can play the fool . . . pretend to be young, but my life is really over . . . 68 years . . . I'll never see them again! Death is on its way to you . . . It is strange that I have been on the stage now for 45 years, and this is the first time I have seen a theatre at night, after the lights have been put out. The first time. [Walks up to the footlights] How dark it is! I can't see a thing . . . Just the prompter's box; the rest is

in pitch darkness, a black, bottomless pit, like a grave, in which death itself might be hiding . . . Brr . . . How cold it is! [Suddenly at far end of stage Svietlovidoff sees Ivanitch, the prompter, an old man, and shrieks with terror] Who are you? What do you want?

It is I, master, Nikita Ivanitch, the prompter . . . I spend my nights here. Please don't tell. I have nowhere else to spend the night.

Ah! It's you, is it? Just think, the audience called me out 16 times; they brought me 3 wreathes; yet not a soul came when it was all over to wake the poor, drunken old man and take him home. I'm old, Nikitushka! Old and ill. [Falls on Ivanitch's neck and weeps] Don't go away. It's time for me to die. It's dreadful!

[Ivanitch tenderly and respectfully tells him it's time to go home]

I won't go there. I have nobody. No one will remember me. Who needs me? Who loves me? Not a soul, Nikitushka.

[Ivanitch, weeping] Your audience loves you, master . . . It is time you went to sleep, sir.

I was a great artist till I threw away my talents, played the fool, lost my looks. I have been swallowed up in that great black pit. But what a genius I was! You cannot imagine the power, eloquence. You cannot imagine how many strings [beats his breast] quivered in this breast! . . . Listen now, wait, let me catch my breath; now listen to this: [Declaims lines from *Boris Godunoff* by Pushkin] Is that bad, eh? Here's something from *King Lear*. The sky is black, see? Rain is pouring down, thunder. Listen: "Blow winds, and crack your cheeks! Rage! Blow! [continues on. Then, impatiently] Now take the part of the Fool. Be quick about it!

[Ivanitch takes the part of the Fool. Together they do a number of lines]

Ah! there is strength, there is talent for you! I'm a great artist! Now take this from *Hamlet*. [Together they do a few dozen lines]

[laughs and claps] Bravo! Encore! Is there any old age in that? Wait a second. Now listen to this tenderness, such music. [Declaims other lines]

[The noise of opening doors is heard. The servants have returned to pick him up and take him home] Let's go, boys. I'm not old! All that is nonsense! [laughs gaily]

[To Ivanitch:] What are you crying for? You poor old granny, you, what's the matter now? Come, come, old man, don't stare so! There, there [embraces Ivanitch in tears] Don't cry! Do you remember those lines from Othello, Nikitushka?

"Farewell the tranquil mind! Farewell content . . . Oh farewell!"

[Ivanitch] Oh! you're a genius, a genius!

And again listen to this:

[they go out together, the curtain falls slowly]

In his dressing-room after the performance, my actor friend: "So how did you like it? Not bad, huh? [hugging, kissing] You *really* liked it? Good! Fine!"

And at the after-show party, he was fully reinflated, prancing, dancing, refilling glasses, performing to lavish applause.

What, then, was the private performance in the sauna? An undress rehearsal? I, a target of opportunity for projection? A refueling stop? A personal confession behind the cover of a rehearsal? A rehearsal under cover of a personal confession? I felt the way a friend of the late Glenn Gould used to feel after late night phone conversations with that pianist: "I found myself acting as an entranced accompanist to a performance, offering a sort of continuo foundation for his improvisations . . . holding forth on any number of . . . subjects . . ." *(New York Times,* October 4, 1992).

Whatever the meanings of this vignette, the essential elements from an analytic point of view are (1) the *absence* in my friend of a reliable *internal* witness to act as a structural factor of internal object constancy, and (2) the *presence* of factors in addition to talent that permitted him to transform this deficit into a successful acting career—instead of, for example, mere repeated externalizations.

Weepers

When Francoise Gilot (Gilot and Lake, 1964, pp. 276–277) and Picasso were living in Vallauris in southern France, their cook, Madame Michel, came to her one evening at six o'clock with a tragic air to say that she had to leave right away because someone was dying in a section nearby and, "In this part of the country nobody dies without me." Since she was not, after all, the village priest, why did she have to leave? "Well, Madame, I'm a weeper; the best weeper in Vallauris. You don't just die, like a dog," she said. "Unless you're very poor, you bring in three weepers to help you get through." She needed no urging to explain further.

> "Well," she said, "when we're called in, the first thing we do is to eat a good meal. Weepers work hard and you can't do that on an empty stomach. Then we draw up our chairs alongside the bed. The main thing is to prolong the agony so that before you leave, you've helped that poor soul recall everything impor-

tant that happened to him all during his life. I might say, 'Do you remember, Ernest, the day of your First Communion, how little Mimi stood behind you and pulled your hair?' I grew up with him, you see, and I remember those things. 'Yes, yes, I remember,' he sobs, and all three of us weepers groan and wail with him. Then it's the next weeper's turn. 'Do you remember the day you left for your military service and how you felt when you had to say good-bye to the family?' If he says yes, then it's the third one's turn, but if he says no, we try it again and again and add more and more details until he does remember. Sometimes, it's a real sad memory, like 'Do you remember, Julie, the time when you lost your little girl from the croup at the age of three?' When Julie cries her heart out, we follow along like a chorus. If it's a happy memory, we all laugh. And it goes on like that through the whole life of the one who's dying."

Gilot said it seemed to her rather gruesome to put someone who was already suffering through an ordeal like that.

"Just the contrary," Madame Michel said. "If he can recall everything of importance that happened to him on earth, happy *or* sad, he can start his new life on the other side happy and free. But it's not as easy as you think. That's why I'm the best weeper around here, because I generally get it all out before they go. Sometimes we have to work fast. Other times, when we can, we take a longer way around, and make things go on like that for two or three days. But the main thing is to make it all come out even. Then, when the poor soul feels the end approaching, he doesn't answer any more; he turns his face to the wall." Madame Michel leaned closer and lowered her voice. "That's more important than extreme unction," she whispered. "Then we eat again and go home. The rest is up to the undertaker" [pp. 276–277].

Next is a final example of a form of external witnessing discourse that, through the agency of an icon, leads to the formation of an internal witness—an internalized object relationship.

Icons

I am indebted to Dr. Dori Laub, cofounder of the Fortunoff Video Archive for Holocaust Testimonies at Yale, for the following story (Felman and Laub, 1992).

> A little boy of about five years old was placed with his parents in . . . a labor camp. A rumor, which eventually materialized, began spreading that all children were going to be rounded up for extermination. . . . One night, while the guards were being distracted . . . his mother wrapped him up in a shawl and gave him a passport photograph of herself as a student. She told him to turn to the picture whenever he felt the need to do so. His parents both promised him that they would come and find him and bring him home after the war. With that, and with an address where to go, he was sent out into the streets. . . . Eventually his hideout became too dangerous and he had to leave. He roamed the streets, joined other gangs of boys and found refuge in the homes of generous, gentile families who took him in for periods of time. The task of making it from day to day preoccupied him completely and in moments of solitude he would take out his mother's picture and talk to her.
>
> In one of the gentile houses he stayed in (living on the papers of a child that had died), the family was in the habit of praying together every evening. When everybody knelt and prayed to the crucifix, the lady of the house, who may have suspected he was Jewish, was kind enough to allow him to pray to whomever he wished. The young boy would take out the photograph of his mother and pray to it, saying, "Mother, let this war be over and come and take me back as you promised." Mother indeed had promised to come and take him back after the war, and not for a moment did he doubt that promise [pp. 86–91].

In Dr. Laub's interpretation, what this young vagabond was doing with the photograph of his mother was, precisely, creating his first witness. The creation of that internal witness was what enabled him to survive physically as well as to create a cohesive, integrated narrative of his life and remain authentic to himself.

> After liberation he manages miraculously to find his parents, but . . . they are not the people he remembers: they no longer even resemble the image he has carried in his mind for so long. His mother does not look like the person in the photograph. His parents have come back as death camp survivors, haggard and emaciated, in striped uniforms, with teeth hanging loose in their gums. Their return does not bring back the lost safety of childhood the boy has so ardently prayed for. He finds that he can only address them as Mr. and Mrs. . . .

To Dr. Laub:

> [T]his story means that in regaining his real mother, he inevitably loses the internal witness he had found in her image. This loss of his internal witness to whom he has addressed his daily prayers causes the boy to fall apart. He begins to have a nightmare that will recur all his life. In it he finds himself on a conveyor belt moving relentlessly . . . to his death. . . . Every time he has this dream, he wakes up, totally disoriented and utterly terrified. Because he has lost . . . the holding presence of a witness, many of the things he consequently does, as he grows up to be a man, are desperate attempts to subdue the abandoned child victim within himself. As a high-ranking officer in the Israeli army he becomes known for repeated acts of bravery. . . . He did not consider them brave at all. They simply partook of his feeling of being invulnerable . . . convinced he could walk in a hail of bullets and not be hit . . . [Denying] the child victim within himself, he becomes instead an untouchable and self-sufficient hero.

Years later, the invitation to give his testimony to the archive at Yale provoked a prolonged crisis within himself. When he finally did so, and established a link to the listener—himself a child survivor of the Holocaust—two things happened. "No longer alone and without a witness, he is able to stop the death machine in his dream without having to wake up . . . [And] for the first time in his life he was able to experience feelings of fear as well."

Being less heroic and more human, he was at last himself.

Another type of "icon" in the form of private prayer is exampled in the life of Anna Larina, the young widow of Nikolai Bukharin, who spent more than twenty years in the Gulag living under frequently savage conditions. One of the main reasons she was able to survive an ordeal that claimed the lives of millions of other Soviet citizens was that she had a secret mission. On the eve of Bukharin's arrest, he made Ms. Larina memorize a final letter-testament entitled, "To a Future Generation of Party Leaders." "He dictated and I repeated it, phrase after phrase. It became my lullaby. When I would fall asleep, I would cover myself up and start mumbling the words" (Larina, 1993, quoted in *The New York Times Book Review*, March 21, 1993, p. 29).

A "witnessing" presence may comprise various degrees of transitional object forms of relatedness extending to and including human empathy. These examples illustrate that the witnessing partners, often animate, may also be inanimate icons.

The Chekhov play and myself unwittingly in the role of Prompter in the play, both illustrate a preestablished literary script and an obligatory social ritual, each of which succeed in providing an infusion of self-esteem through favorable external mirroring. The "weepers" work to recall and relive personal shared memories, thereby relieving a degree of pressure from accumulated private affects. The photograph acts as an "icon" that provides a vital illusion: there exists an internal witness to a covenant that all in the end will be well.

The psychoanalytic, I suggest, is another "witnessing" relationship—unique in its attempt to invite *internal* factors as far as possible, the better to clarify and interpret the extent to which they permeate one's reality. One bears witness to a patient's verbal testimony, allowing each person's speech in the privileged psychoanalytic situation to disclose what had been essentially unavailable to its own speaker. Treatment becomes the safe external playground to experience—perhaps for the first time—or to reexperience, neutralize, distance, and discharge dangerous affects; where, above all, the opportunity exists to create that safe, workable, inner space in which there is both room to breathe and separate, and be witnessed and supported.

Analysts are not "prompters," "weepers," or "icons." Moreover, we have the assurance of a body of theory that allots central importance to insight and working through—including insight and working through of the analytic relationship itself, both real and transferential, together with due allowance for countertransference in its valuable and negative aspects.

As in the examples cited, emotion is central to the entire enterprise, yet psychoanalytic affect theory is still struggling to clarify its relationship to the hypothetical sources of energy (Sandler, 1987). And despite recent progress in neuroscience, we still have no key to translate the language of neurophysiology into that of psychology (Reiser, 1984).

We may well seek elsewhere. Just as the dream is the traditional royal road to the unconscious, we may say, on the basis of developmental psychology, that affect is the royal road of entry from outside to inside in that it is the first and most fundamental response to the dynamic qualities of reality; that is to say, the patterns of tension and release either inherent in the outside world or imputed to it. These are the very qualities that art highlights. Therefore, we are led to explore the emotional resonances to art for clues to the nature of both art and affect.

Perhaps not surprisingly, a dream image brings a first glimpse of some of the relationships involved.

> *A volcanic island upthrusted nightly from the deep,*
> *to be lost with each dawn's flood of dailiness.*

Is art that island, recaptured from dream, cultivated and rendered accessible, to live always in the dance and play of the surf and tides of affect?

2

FROM DREAMING
TO CREATIVE VISION,
TOWARD FORMS AND FEELING

A patient began his regular session in his usual way. He lay down on the couch and after a somewhat longer pause than customary began: "I had a strange dream last night. It seems there were seven fat cows and seven lean cows . . ."

We both laughed at his teasing. But since we both knew that jokes are no simple laughing matter, at least in analysis, we learned in time that his "dream-joke" was offering a deal and a challenge—an offer to share some of his unconscious grandiosity with me: his dreams, like that of an Egyptian Pharaoh's, contained hidden revelations requiring the interpretive talents of no one less than a Joseph.

This chapter was adapted and expanded from "From Dreams to Creative Vision: Toward Affect Theory." In: *The Spectrum of Psychoanalysis. Essays in Honor of Martin Bergmann* (1994). A. K. Richards and A. D. Richards, Editors. Madison, CT: International Universities Press.

12

Ancient tradition connects dreaming and revelation. Sometimes it included a privileged place for insanity as well—a notion that goes back to Dionysiac rites. This literary heritage extends from the fifth century B.C. to the present time (L. Feder, 1980). It peaks in the romantic literary and artistic movements of the late eighteenth and nineteenth centuries. In revolt against strict adherence to reason and intellect, artists and writers turned instead to passionate emotional expressiveness and sensuousness for inspiration. If one happened to be self-centered, absentminded, or a touch "mad," this went with the territory: being a creative artist (or scientist) meant being a "Dreamer of Dreams," a seer.

Romanticism held that consciousness had been so restricted for millennia by accretions of rationality that it had become alienated from its own true nature; it could be liberated only by a return (or rebirth), to the eternal roots that lay below the crusts and lies of "civilization." Romanticism expressed a yearning to merge with the universe. It embraced Nietzsche's "Dionysian state" of boundlessness between self and symbols, representations, actual persons, places and events—an eternal "Yes and Amen." Since mystical yearning alone and unchecked would lead ultimately to death, individual existence required the safeguard of Nietzsche's "Apollonian" life principle to impose differentiation upon the chaos and mold it into form, order, beauty.

Surrealism applied these ideas to the area of visual imagery. Its aim was to "free" the unconscious mind, resolve the apparent contradictions between dream and reality, and thus create a kind of absolute reality—a surreality. A hitherto unknown territory of sensuous imagination lay in one's unconscious depths awaiting liberation. The way to facilitate its emergence was not through some kind of self-indulgence; rather, the royal road was through patient, deliberate, and systematic confusion and disorder of the senses, automatisms, and creatively reordering visual images from dreams.

Even before Freud discovered a key to the unconscious in this treasurehouse of images, a professor of chemistry in Ghent made the most important dream interpretation since Joseph deciphered Pharaoh's—that of the seven fat and seven lean cows. While dozing before the fire, Friedrich von Kekulé had a mental vision of long rows of twining and twisting snakelike structures. "But look! What was that? One of the snakes had seized hold of its own tail, and the form whirled mockingly before my eyes. As if by a flash of lightning I awoke . . . Let us learn to dream, gentlemen" (quoted from Findlay [1948, pp. 36–38]).

The key that von Kekulé found in the dream was not the Freudian one that could unlock the door to the dream's latent content leading into the unconscious. Rather, he made an immediate connection to the day's residue of conscious and preconscious preoccupations having to do with images of molecules. The autophagous snake suggested the ring structure of the benzene molecule, and thereby established one cornerstone of modern science.

The dream, of course, provides two doors: one leading upwards and the other downwards. Had he been in analysis, von Kekulé might have found that the image of the snake with its tail in its mouth was a symbolic reference to autofellatio, perhaps thus accounting for both the (sexual) twining and twisting as well as its "mocking" him. He may have gone on to discover that the autofellatio formation itself was a multilayered expressive vehicle for sexual and aggressive drives and their related objects (Orland, 1971); that an image of autofellatio had been noted in connection with scientific inventiveness (Lorand, 1934); that it was one of the secret Tantric Buddhist methods of redirecting sexual energy from the genitals to the brain for the purpose of enlightenment (Woods [1987, p. 21], citing Allegro [1977, p. 109]). *But*, although the autoerotic image can refer to the creative process of reaching deeply into oneself, actual attempts at autofellatio are practiced not only by the fictional Alex Portnoy but also by "a considerable portion of the population . . . at least in early adolescence" (Kinsey, Pomeroy, and Martin, 1948, p. 510)—*without* any known correlation to subsequent creativity.

The point is that for von Kekulé, at least, the thrust of the image was not "downwards"—to climax in a (perhaps) universal pool of sexual fantasy. Rather, it was toward conscious and preconscious visual imagery, making possible an original linkage between two totally disparate realms.

One may suppose that, at the instant of awakening or just before, he must have been able to make use of two different kinds of perception: a wide-ranging, fluidly merging, holistic, or imaginative, primary process type of perception in combination with a sharply focused, realistic, secondary process type of perception that delineates clear boundaries. The latter "knows" that a snake has both mouth and tail, *and* that atoms form molecular chains; the former overlooks the *differences*, sees mainly the elements of *sameness*, and perhaps energized by an unconscious sexual fantasy, conflates snake and molecule, thrusting the "tail" of the molecule into its "mouth." The interplay of primary and secondary process perception has transformed the idea of molecular chains into the concept of molecular rings, creating a vision for a new era in chemistry.

Let us look more closely at the interplay of primary and secondary processes in the dream. Being less encumbered by the reality constraints of the secondary process, the primary process mechanisms of condensation and displacement can equate here and there, now and then, near and far; objects float, combine, separate, recombine; opposites coexist; structures are unstable and boundaries are fluid. The dreamer samples the primary process ferment that normally underlies the conscious, secondary process type of perception. On awakening, most dreams are successfully repressed and forgotten or, if remembered, secondarily revised; or signal anxiety develops and the dreamer awakens; or the dream is otherwise short-circuited in line with the primary process tendency for immediate discharge.

That is what happened in the following dream. Before doing so, however, it provided a glimpse of the traffic amongst all the agencies of the mind as well as the primary and secondary process modes of perception.

Not long after the death of his father a man dreamed that he and his older sister—a mother figure to him in many ways—were at the site of an ancient cemetery. It was high up on the side of a hill and they used to hike there on summer vacations, wander among the old stones, and try to make out the epitaphs and their dates. In the dream there they were again. The view of the valley and the mountain beyond was as beautiful and peaceful as he remembered it. He picked up a leaded glass window that was lying at his feet, held it up in front of him and looked through the window at the panorama. It now appeared to lie immediately at hand and around him *while at the same time* it was far below and beyond. He was simultaneously inside and outside the scene. "It certainly is beautiful," he said, "but much too far to commute!" Whereupon he burst out laughing—and awoke.

Let us briefly summarize some of the issues embedded in the dream imagery. Alone with sister: oedipal; *ancient* cemetery: emphasis is shifted away from mourning father's *recent* death; breastlike hills: defensive regression to pre-oedipal material; conflation of near and far: the fearful awareness of the *finiteness* of time and thus the inevitability of death is converted into the *boundlessness* of space.

The emphatic beauty of the scene attempts to transform many kinds of intense feelings, as well as anxiety about the passage from life to death, into something aesthetic and transcendental. Nevertheless, anxiety threatened to break through. Primary process condensed life and death and, linking up with secondary process knowledge of commutation, created a defensive joke: loss is not irrevocable and death is no scary one-way trip but a two-way commute. Anxiety was only partially defused and the dreamer awoke. The burst of laughter is typical primary process immediate discharge.

Typical of the primary process mode of visual organization is the experience of being both inside and outside the scene of hills and valleys far below and also immediately at hand. This was a pictorial means of representing the idea of commuting between heaven and earth. On the face of it, this equation of dying with being born is a ludicrous thought fit for a joke or a religious nostrum. But also, let it be noted, the stuff of poetic metaphor. In a stunning image, Samuel Beckett (1951) compounds the awesomeness of dying with that of birthing: "for already from the world that parts at last its labia and lets me go" (p. 189).

The dream, being transparent, renders the interplay of primary and secondary process modes of organizing sensory data clearly apparent. To the extent that art knowingly accesses and stimulates their interplay there may be some basis for the ancient, if romantic, notion of a special relationship existing between dream and creative process. Beyond that, both may be viewed as lenses that magnify and slow down the operations of the mind as they integrate conscious surface with unconscious depth. But the dream passes into oblivion having assimilated a private real event with the universal unconscious. Art, while undoubtedly having roots in the unconscious, reaches upward to the shared world of conscious and preconscious attention and perception, transforming it more or less enduringly.

Of course, scientific investigation of the world, like artistic exploration, also expands our awareness. That is why scholarly tradition going back as far as the Renaissance has viewed them as complementary to each other. There is, however, an important subjective emotional distinction to be made between them—important as it bears on the way art "works."

While von Kekulé's creative intellectual vision resulted in a conceptual discovery, creative aesthetic vision succeeds in reintegrating affect with thought and perception (Rose, 1987). This makes experience "come alive" with fresh sensuousness and emotion. This is to be distinguished from the *emotion* von Kekulé undoubtedly had in response to the flash of insight resulting from the "bisociation" or melding of two different "matrices" (Koestler, 1964). The knowledge of the benzene ring is unlikely to afford anyone else an emotional experience apart, perhaps, from identifying with von Kekulé and the private emotion that undoubtedly accompanied *his* moment of intellectual illumination.

If an artist were to depend on a similar type of "bisociation" as in visual punning, for example, he would be inventive at best or, at worst, "gimmicky." Despite the surrealist conceit about breaking through the constraints of reality to a revolutionary new realm of surreality, such a device by itself might carry an initial shock value but a brief half-life before becoming a footnote of art history.

In contrast to a dream which gives only a glimpse of the ferment of primary and secondary process interplay underlying all perception, and then a short circuit discharge and quick curtain, art often captures it and raises it from subliminal into full awareness. Instead of subordinating primary to secondary process perception as in daily life, or the reverse as in dreaming, art raises both to a state of near balance. This brings them to a level of prolonged and, more important, feelingful awareness. (For a detailed discussion in respect to Picasso, cf. Rose [1980]; and on Monet, cf. Rose [1987].) For an aesthetically sensitive audience, creative aesthetic vision carries a lasting *emotional* valence that transforms everyday perception and emotional dulling into an expanded apprehension of reality. Thus various artists, celebrating the infinite qualities of light, for example, "rescue" them from habitual inattention and restore them to *feelingful awareness.*

This is the subject to which we now turn.

In 1926 Marion Milner began a diary about "my excitement in discovering that I could deliberately use two different kinds of perception (with startlingly different results) one being what I called wide-focused on purpose, as against my normal narrow focused kind. In those days I never thought in terms of Freud's primary and secondary process" (personal communication, November 20, 1989).

One can easily guess the reason it was not possible "in those days" to think of these two interpenetrating forms of attention and perception in terms of primary and secondary process. Psychoanalysis, under the influence of nineteenth century physiology, was operating on the basis of a closed system model of the organism. In *The Interpretation of Dreams,* Freud (1900, p. 603) had postulated that the primary and secondary processes were in fundamental opposition to each other: the secondary process must attain "domination" over the "falsification" of the primary process. Even though this might not take place until the prime of life, "a sharp and final decision" between these two modes should take place by puberty (Freud, 1915, p. 195).

Having always been interested in learning how to paint, Milner (1957) discovered almost against her will—because it seemed to threaten familiar beliefs about the superiority of realistic willpower and conscious effort—that it was possible to surpass her previous uncertain efforts by giving equal validity to these two different modes of attention and permit a cyclic oscillation to take place between them.

She found on the one hand that a narrow-focus type of surface attention keeps trying to force what happens into a preconceived idea or pattern; on the other hand, a kind of absent-minded, receptive watchfulness goes on during the gaps in one's surface attention. This latter is complementary to and a corrective for a too rigid adherence to the commonsensical consensus that orders our daily lives. Using both in conjunction with each other is a way of making use of a creative relation to one's unconscious. One discovers "the sense in nonsense" and becomes better able to "order the chaos."

At just about the same time Milner began her diary about two different kinds of attention, Lev Semonovich Vygotsky, a Soviet scholar, wrote (1931) *The Psychology of Art* (translated [1971]). (I am grateful to Lisa Reese for placing it in my hands.) While the book deals with literature, its subject has to do with the problem of how some writing manages to rise above the semantic value of words to become feelingful art. Literature, of course, "works" with human feelings, but how does a literary *artist* transform feelings so that they transcend the author's private, personal domain? He explicitly rejects the formula "communication of feelings" as simplistic—a view that by now appears well established.

Through an analysis of literary structure, Vygotsky discerns a "movement of opposite feelings" that intersect and culminate in a *catharsis*. By this he has in mind neither an

Aristotelian nor a Freudian meaning. He refers, rather, to an emotional response to art that is elevated to a nonpersonal plane and embraces within itself the immediacy of a revealed knowledge of a more general human truth.

Such transcendence aside, however, how is one to elucidate the emotional response to art? Vygotsky turns to Darwin's *The Expression of Emotions in Man and Animals* (1872). There, Darwin postulates that moods cause certain habitual movements which may be regarded as useful; opposite moods involve an involuntary tendency to perform movements of an opposite nature which seem useless. Opposing impulses are associated with an involuntary performance of opposing movements at the same time.

The aesthetic response, according to Vygotsky, similarly embodies contradiction, one that reflects an intimate conflict in the artistic structure itself. Since literature is his focus, he locates the internal struggle as taking place between content and form, with the latter achieving victory over the former and, in fact, "destroy[ing]" (p. 215) it.

It would be more consistent, as well as making the idea of conflict at the heart of aesthetic structure applicable to nonverbal art as well as literature, to say—as, indeed, he does elsewhere—that the distinction between form and content becomes obliterated in art. Content in art is embodied in form; as structure carries function, and function expresses structure, each penetrates the other.

However, the idea of contrary movements taking place within aesthetic structure is a valuable one and the point to which he applies it at the conclusion of his argument is apposite to our present purpose. It has to do with imagination versus the knowledge of reality. The imaginative illusion of reality stimulates motor impulses while the knowledge of reality inhibits and delays the motor expression. It is this collision of opposite impulses that "initiates an explosive discharge of nervous energy . . . which culminates in the discharge of emotions" (p. 215).

Imagination versus knowledge of reality. These everyday kitchenware terms serve admirably to distinguish the salient features of primary and secondary processes. Recall Marion Milner's two different kinds of attention: the absent-minded, diffuse watchfulness and the narrow-focus type of surface attention. Further, that giving them equal validity and permitting a cyclic oscillation between them resulted in an improvement in the quality of her paintings.

Of course! She was inviting a free flow between imaginative and knowledgeable perception. The former allowed entree into consciousness of the various primary process modes of organizing sensory data, free from the tension of nose-to-the-grindstone attention to details and boundaries. At the same time, alert, high energy, knowledgeable perception brought some sense to the nonsense and conventional order to the chaos. The cyclic oscillation between the two modes revealed an *un*common sense in nonsense and a new creative order.

Psychoanalytic approaches now emphasize that, whether or not one deliberately invites and explores such an interplay of wide and narrow focus (as one does in free-floating analytic attention or artistic endeavors), there *is* a continuum between *primary process imagination* and *secondary process knowledge of reality*. They *do* interact on all levels, are not sharply distinguishable, and they impart qualities of both spontaneity and control. This has been a major theoretical shift that has been taking place within psychoanalysis: from a closed to an open system model of the organism. One important implication is that we can now take a different view of the nature of sublimation. We can begin to see it as more than just another ego defense, albeit with redeeming social value. Rather, it begins to come into its own as a significant means of promoting ego strength and expanding the appreciation of reality (Rose, 1980, 1987, 1990, 1991).

Returning now to Vygotsky and his idea that a collision of contrary motions lies behind aesthetic *e*-motion. Like Milner's discussion of two different types of perception, this too may be comfortably subsumed in an open system interplay between primary process imaginative perception and secondary process knowledgeable perception. The oscillation of "contrary motions" between imaginative and knowledgeable perception generates a flux of tension and release. Tension is associated with focused attention and perception; release of tension with a flow in the opposite direction toward a free-floating attention and absent-minded yet watchful perception.

Now it is precisely tension-release, either in quantitative terms or in the form, possibly, of rhythmic changes of stimulus strength, that Freud (1915, 1924) speculated might be at the core of pleasure-unpleasure. This in turn comes to constitute the matrix of emotion, which particular emotion, depending on the conscious and unconscious ideas that have come to be associated with it in the course of time (Brenner, 1974).

Since every art form may be viewed as an energy system involving tension and release, it is now possible to spell out the relation between the tension-release structure of aesthetic form and an individual's personal emotional response: the intensified and directed interplay of sensuous forms in the art stimulates heightened sensations of pleasure and unpleasure, and arouses each person's *resonating* personal associations and individual emotions.

By seeking out and elaborating perceptual rhythms of tension and release, art highlights the emotionally expressive valence of experience. The artist or composer must discover how the patterns of attraction and repulsion among the various visual or acoustic elements he has selected can be intensified so that an audience, experiencing the energic flux of tension and release, can grasp the rhythms of forces making up the structure.

Since the purpose of this chapter is to present an overview, only a few general examples will suffice. Bach's "Art of the Fugue" is said to have been built according to the principles of constructivism, an idea handed down from medieval times that music is essentially a mathematical discipline. Thus, Leibniz: "Music is a secret exercise of arithmetic during which the mind is unaware that it is counting."

While being "constructivist," however, "The Art of the Fugue" is written in the undeviating key of D-Minor around a single theme based on a minor triad with narrow intervals around it. These elements practically amount to a formula for conveying pathos. Thus, the rational principle of mathematicallike constructivism is joined with highly emotional musical material to form a mutual tension of ratio and pathos.

For examples in visual art we may turn to the contrasting ways in which Western and Chinese art are said to deal with opposing tensions. Art historians (Rowley, 1947) tell us that Christianity and Hellenic thought molded Western art in such a way as to set up antagonistic dualisms: classic-romantic, divine-human, matter-spirit, traditional-progressive, ideal-natural, and so on. Each extreme was pursued to its end.

In contrast, Chinese views of life—both Taoism and Confucianism—characteristically espouse the idea of a dynamic union of opposites which need each other for completeness. This is embedded in Chinese painting where one finds an equilibrium of opposites such as expansion and constriction, movement and tension. Movement needs resting tension lest it become all flux; resting tension needs movement lest it degenerate into static balance. The artist must be neither classic nor romantic, he should be both; his painting must be neither naturalistic nor idealistic, it must be both; his style must be neither traditional nor original, it must be both. Chinese art resides somewhere between the Western extremes. It provides a fluid field for the interaction of forces and the endless expansion of nuance.

Whether a Western-style antagonistic dualism or a Chinese type of dynamic equilibrium, the significant point for our purpose is that the structure of art embodies patterns of tension and release at its core. The sensitivity to patterns of tension and release constitutes the expressive quality of perception: the capacity to perceive with feeling. It is the most elementary attribute of perception—the primary content of vision (Arnheim, 1954, p. 430). And it connects art to biology.

The justification for this statement is the fact that a biological task of the organism's perceptual apparatus is to make an immediate practical appraisal of any new situation. What are its vibes—its perceived friendliness or hostility? And what's to do: Approach? Withdraw? Remain watchful? Perceiving with feeling depends on responding to the dynamic aspects of reality—sights and sounds, for example, in terms of their dynamic qualities as forces of directed tensions.

Given a biological basis for the expressive quality of perception, it is understandable that it is probably hard-wired in the central nervous system. In infancy, not only do thought and perception appear to be intertwined with emotion, but memory also seems to be involved from the outset as part of a total experience. Accumulating research suggests that nonverbal memories are registered subcortically (LeDoux, Romanski, and Xagoraris, 1989). Adrenaline and noradrenaline, secreted under the influence of emotion, can boost the registration of memories in proportion to the emotional charge (Cahill et al., 1994). Since stimulation runs along the same or parallel circuits serving affects, sensations, and memory functions, and since there are connecting shunts between these pathways, memories trigger feelings and vice versa, as clinical experience shows—and Proust long knew.

Developmental psychology is also providing detailed information as to how an infant's caretakers, universally and intuitively, seem to cultivate the expressive quality of perception from the very beginning. There is also some evidence that certain characteristic dynamic expressive forms of specific qualities in various sensory modes—for example, sentient shapes of motoric pressure and release—may have the direct power to induce specific emotions without the necessity for symbolic transformations. It appears that the infant, in the course of intuitive play, handling, and other daily interactions with the earliest caretakers, learns to generalize and displace these dynamic expressive motoric patterns to other sensory realms such as sight and sound (cf. Chapter 5).

The expressive quality of perception, then, refers to basic, subjective affective responsivity to objective sentient patterns of tension and release. *Forms of feeling* may thus be construed in this double sense: objective sentient patterns of tension and release as well as the subjective affective response to them by molding perception and cognition into a systematic feelingful awareness of reality.

For greater clarity, we will henceforth refer to the former, the objective patterns of tension and release in art, as apparent "attunement"; and the latter, the subjective response, as "emotional resonances" (cf. Chapter 5).

Returning a final time to Vygotsky, he cites Tolstoy on the precise fine-tuning between aesthetic form and emotional response. Tolstoy tells an anecdote about the Russian painter Briullov because, Tolstoy writes:

> [it shows] better than anything else, . . . what can and what cannot be taught at school. As he was correcting the sketch of a pupil, Briullov gave it a few touches here and there, and the dull, drab sketch suddenly came to life. "But you've *scarcely* touched it, and everything has changed!" said one of the pupils. "Art begins where *scarcely* starts," replied Briullov, expressing the most characteristic trait of . . . all the arts. . . . It occurs to the degree and extent in which the artist finds those infinitesimal elements which make up his work. There is no way to teach . . . how to discover . . . these elements . . . This can be achieved only by feeling [Tolstoy, *Collected Works*, Vol. 30, Moscow, 1951, pp. 127–128].

Vygotsky concludes: "'Art begins where *scarcely* starts' is tantamount to saying that art begins where form begins . . . The starting point without which the understanding of art is impossible, is the emotion of form" (1971, p. 37).

To this we may now add: "emotion of form" is a way of referring to sentient patterns of tension and release that elicit a responsive *resonance* of corresponding tension and release experienced subjectively as emotion. Kris (1952) alluded to this bodily reaction as a specific component of the aesthetic response. In describing the slight kinesthetic reaction which one experiences on looking long enough at a painting or sculpture of the human figure, he wrote: "From looking at a whirl of lines, from following them, we change imperceptibly from identification with the model into the stage in which we 'imitate' the strokes and lines with which it was produced . . . Art critics seem to have repeatedly hinted at the existence of a similar mechanism" (p. 56).

It is instructive that, in making this cogent observation, Kris made no allusion to emotion. In fact, "affect," "feeling," and "emotion" do not appear in the index of his seminal work. At this remove, one may suggest that the emerging importance of emotion in psychoanalytic psychology has been concurrent with a growing appreciation of (1) the ego's role in adaptation and in maintaining the homeostasis of feeling states; and (2) the central importance of the holding environment of the infant/caretaker relationship.

It is in the context of the latter that patterns of sentient stimulation of pleasure and unpleasure take place, the earliest sense of self begins to arise, and self and object representations become more clearly delineated. Precursors of affect, in close relationship to the earliest sense of self, probably constitute the original motivational system. The concordant or dissonant qualities of the holding environment provide the sentient matrix for two basic transformations: internalization and sublimation (cf. Chapter 6).

This increasing status of emotions in analytic theory toward a position of primacy was prefigured by the Kleinians (Stein, 1991). They insisted early on that the psyche constantly endeavors to concretize feelings and form internal objects out of them to relate to through fantasies and storytelling. In other words, emotions come first and fantasies are elaborated to tell their story (Riviere, 1936; Isaacs, 1943; Klein, M., 1957, p. 88).

Perhaps the lag in giving due theoretical recognition to emotion was because of the primacy accorded to fantasy and early thought, both being wedded presumably to the beginnings of verbalization at about eighteen months. Now, however, it becomes possible to speculate about infantile mental organization prior to the capacity for verbalization at about eighteen months. Still closer to our purpose, it becomes feasible to theorize about the emotional response to nonverbal abstract art, and to do so without having to postulate the existence of unconscious (verbal) fantasies, let alone the *communication* of these as assumed to occur between an author and a receptive reader.

For example, ideally one would expect that average expectable degrees of perceptual-affecto-motor arousal would be contained by the early holding environment. Since ideal conditions cannot prevail consistently, there will be spikes of stimulation as well as prolonged states of arousal *not* contained by the holding environment. When fantasy and verbalization do become available, they can help bind this excessive tension *retroactively* by imposing a cognitive structure of "explanatory" plausibility by way of narrative coherence.

Nonverbal, nonrepresentational abstract art including music knowingly *stimulates* and at the same time *contains* a concentrated range of perceptual, affective and motoric elements. Such art may be clued into preverbal emotional memories before there is a capacity to enlist fantasy to help bind stress retroactively. Viewed developmentally, it could represent ongoing attempts to bring into a self-contained and perhaps new kind of balance degrees and types of stimulation that would have exceeded the capacity of one's earlier self to contain. In addition to possibly reflecting this kind of unbound early stress, in common with all art it mobilizes the need to respond to the challenge of new stimulation. This includes the adaptive use of fantasy secondarily when this becomes available.

What is the place of veridicity and fantasy in such a schema? The veridicity that makes up the aesthetic illusion is inherent in the formal congruence between patterns of tension and release in the structure of art and in the core dynamic of feelings. It may be considered primary in that it is this congruence that initiates a person's responsive emotional resonances. Susan Langer puts it this way: "The establishment and organization of tensions is the basic technique in projecting the image of feeling, the artist's idea, in any medium. . . . [It leads to] an isomorphy of actual organic tensions and virtual . . . created tensions . . ." (Langer, 1967, p. 164).

The artist will have created the conditions for the aesthetic illusion of veridicity: a perceived identity between actual and virtual tensions. This may be inseparable from an accompanying fantasy of a responsive emotional presence—a fantasy probably rooted in preverbal memories of the holding environment. It facilitates the creation by a recipient of any number of individual further fantasies as personally needed, whether of oedipal or preoedipal content, and irrespective of any "communication" by the author of his or her own.

At this stage in the history of psychoanalysis art does not have to be just another area like primitive myth and neurotic symptom to round up the usual suspects for unconscious fantasy and conflict resolution in disguise. These operations by now may be considered ubiquitous. A contemporary analytic study of art can begin to include abstract art and music in the expectation that they might generate fresh perspectives on the significance of art and psychoanalysis for each other. Foremost among these are that art can contribute to the analytic understanding of affect; and psychoanalysis can throw light on the potential role of art in emotional development.

Having begun with elucidating the dream in relation to the past and the Unconscious, psychoanalysis faces the challenge of exploring the nature of affect as the first and most fundamental response to the dynamic quality of reality.

3

PAUL GAUGUIN
THROUGH THE LOOKING GLASS

*To me a picture is a window that looks out
on something, the question is–on what?*
—André Breton

*If one looks at a thing . . . trying to
discover what it means, one ends
up no longer seeing the thing itself
but thinking of the question.*
—René Magritte

The space between Breton's question and Magritte's caution traces a dilemma and a challenge. Let us approach it with the help of a metaphor.

Imagine a two-way mirror—sometimes more opaque, sometimes less. Let it represent a creative system: the artist on one side, the audience on the other, an artwork in

This chapter was adapted and expanded from "Paul Gauguin: Art, Androgyny, and the Fantasy of Rebirth" (1990). In: *The Homosexualities. Reality, Fantasy, and the Arts*, pp. 259–270, edited by C. W. Socarides and V. D. Volkan. New York: International Universities Press.

31

between. Suppose that the artist transmits personal, even private, thoughts, feelings, observations, memories, into an intermediate area lying somewhere between the subjective and the objective; and thence is able to transform them into an impersonal, perhaps abstract realm from which an attuned recipient "creates" one's own feelingful mixture of subjective and objective responses.

Consider Paul Gauguin, looking into a fresh canvas as "mirror" to some of his thoughts, observations, memories—and underlying feelings, as we infer them from his life and work—"dreaming" on them and transforming them into his art.

Is it fair to expect that a creative person's work might tell us something about that person? Yes and no—depending on whatever the medium—whether poetry, photography, or whatever—depending on the artist's intention, the tradition in which he or she works, and the individual style.

Expressionists, ancient (Grunewald) or modern, emphasize emotional force—whether personal (Van Gogh), abstract rhythms (Cezanne), or rich color effects (Gauguin). Many poured their personal lives into their work (Munch, Picasso) and offer abundant material for responsible psychoanalytic exploration—when supported by supplementary documentation. Or wild speculation. (For a recent critique of the latter, see Esman [1994], on Pollock's "psychoanalytic" drawings.)

On the other hand, many artists work in a tradition that emphasizes verisimilitude and fidelity to a well-defined iconography and technique. They have chosen to subordinate the personal as far as possible in the service of an aesthetic or, in earlier times, a religious ideal. The contemporary Frank Stella: "What you see is what you see." Obviously, there is little to hang an interpretation on—except defensiveness.

And for artists of whatever stripe, a point too often neglected in the past by psychoanalysts is the importance of the implicit "conversation" through their work, whether through overt reference, repartee, or other means, with the relevant art historical background as it interacts with the development of their own style. The emphasis on realism and tradition will work against the artwork being a *decipherable* "witness" to its *author's* experience, however a particular observer on the other side of the two-way mirror may happen to "resonate" to it.

This chapter has a twofold purpose. The one that takes up the bulk of the text follows a traditional format: it traces a particular theme in Gauguin's art—androgyny—and suggests how, together with fantasies of rebirth, these may have played a significant role in his personal and creative life. That is, they may have helped to organize forms that mirror and transform currents of feeling.

Once sublimated into art, however, they serve to induce and reflect a recipient's *own* feelings and perhaps his *own* personal fantasies, which may or may not coincide with androgyny or rebirth. Thus, the second purpose is to downplay the significance of this or, by implication, any other mental content lying behind the artist's impetus for the work, for the *recipient's* aesthetic, emotional resonances.

The theme of androgyny and fantasies of rebirth follows a psychoanalytic trail first begun by Macalpine and Hunter (1953). Differing from Freud in the Schreber case, they argued that the wish to have the characteristics of the other sex in addition to one's own was intrinsically ego syntonic and formed one mainspring of human activity and creativity in both sexes.

The following year Erikson (1954) wrote: "The creative individual . . . identif[ies] with father, mother and newborn child all in one; . . . represent[ing] in equal measure, his father's potency, his mother's fertility, and his own *reborn* ideal identity" (p. 49; emphasis added). In 1961, Rose wrote: The "artist . . . expresses an omnipotent, hermaphroditic fantasy whose roots lie deep in identification with the pre-oedipal, phallic mother as well as the biological anlage of bisexuality" (p. 548). More recently (Oremland, 1985), the theme of hermaphrodism and creativity has once again been taken up in a study of Michelangelo's *Ignudi* on the Sistine Chapel ceiling.

The idea of androgyny or hermaphrodism is well known in mythology. Hermaphroditus, for example, the son of Aphrodite and Hermes, was a shy youth of 15. When he attempted to resist a nymph's embrace and kisses, she cried out to the gods that they grant that nothing should ever separate him from her or her from him. Immediately their two bodies became joined as one. In their double form they were neither man nor woman, of no sex, yet of both.

From the time of classical antiquity there has been a tradition that held up the androgyne or hermaphrodite as a distinct type of ideal beauty—a person of either ambiguous gender or appropriate to a homoerotic context. Conflating androgyny, effeminacy, and homosexuality, literary and artistic sources from classical times to the Renaissance developed an image of a figure that combined feminine body contours and breasts together with male genitalia. Today this might be categorized as bisexual rather than homosexual.

This ambiguous image of the androgyne, representing the union of masculine and feminine traits in one individual, is sufficiently complex that, historically, it underwent two contrasting developments: on the one hand it came to stand for intensified, bisexual or indiscriminate eroticism; on the other hand, the idea of fused opposites within one being became the source of a long literary and artistic tra-

dition signifying desexualized self-containment and a transcendence over sexual desire. Leonardo, for example, is said
to have subordinated all his emotions to the search for a
timeless, unearthly, unified peacefulness of a single androgynous being such as the one he depicted in his *St. John.*
Such a fascination with primordial unity that transcends
sexuality is also found among the late Greek Hermetic philosophers and early Christian Gnostics as well as the alche-
mists and Renaissance Neoplatonists (Saslow, 1986).

In contrast to the diverse aspects that characterized the
complex development of the idea of androgyny, the psychoanalytic view of dreams and fantasies that combine the characteristics of both sexes has been singularly one-dimensional.
With few exceptions, the psychoanalytic literature usually
describes this as a derivative of unconscious homosexual
drives. Yet, as Kubie (1974) pointed out, the drive to become
both sexes is not identical with genital homosexuality; it has
ingredients from every stage of psychosexual development
and becomes reactivated repeatedly at every stage of life including during the aging process; indeed, it "radiate[s] in
subtle ways into almost every aspect of our culture and par-
ticularly throughout the creative arts" (p. 358).

Within such a context, namely, that the androgynous fantasy is easily reactivated and has far-ranging interconnec-
tions with many stages and levels of development, one may
assume that a linkage also exists with homosexuality. Leaving aside whether or not there is a particular affinity between the drive to become both sexes and homosexuality,
a possible connection between them might be by way of
rebirth fantasies.

Glauber (1937) implied as much when he pointed to the
central position of rebirth fantasies in the multiple causa-
tion of homosexuality. In a prescient glimpse into some of
the dynamically shifting equilibria of the growth process,

he went on to relate rebirth fantasies both with "downward" and "upward" movements [my terms]: accompanying efforts to regain a mother–child symbiosis on the one hand, and on the other, attempts to dissolve it in a thrust toward individuation. It is my own sense that an alternating rhythm of regression and progression, accompanied by fantasies of rebirth, is a frequent *concomitant* of growth, analysis, and the creative process (Rose, 1980, 1987).

Gauguin–Some Biographical Data

Paul Gauguin's grandmother, Flora Tristan, was a fiery socialist who worked for the cause of working people. The illegitimate daughter of a poor Frenchwoman and an aristocratic Spanish colonialist from Peru, she left her husband while pregnant with her second child and went to Peru seeking a share of her paternal inheritance. Her husband tried to kill her, kidnapped their daughter, Aline, the future mother of Paul Gauguin, tried to rape her, and was imprisoned for seventeen years. Aline, as gentle, sad, and grieving at 19 (in a description by George Sand) as her mother was violent, married a newspaperman, Clovis Gauguin. The couple had a daughter and then a son, Paul. Unemployed at the time of Paul's birth, the father was absent from the baptism. He died at sea in somewhat mysterious circumstances while en route with the family to Peru. Paul was just under 17 months of age. Mother and the two children lived with a great-uncle in Lima until Paul was 6 and then returned to France. The children were supported by a trust fund set up by the Peruvian grandfather; mother worked as a seamstress.

When Paul was 17 his mother drew up a will in which she suggested to her son that he "get on with his career, since he has made himself so unliked by all my friends that he will one day find himself alone." For the next five years Gauguin was in the merchant marine and in the military service. He then went to work as a stockbroker, married a Danish bourgeoise, and had four children. After the stock-market crash of 1882 he hesitated between art and finance for two years. Finally, when his fifth child was born, he gave him his own name, Paul, and listed himself on his son's birth certificate as "artist-painter."

When this youngest child was one and a half years old, almost exactly his own age when his *father*, Clovis, died at sea, painter Paul suddenly took *son* Clovis and left his wife to support herself as best she could by giving French lessons and doing translations. Not long afterwards, he left son Clovis stranded in a boarding school in Paris and went to Brittany.

This pattern suggests that the drama of father's death was reenacted, corrected, and recorrected in the form of successive departures: reenacted in that baby Paul is left by father, painter Paul, at the same age that the latter had been left by his own father's death; corrected in that this time father does not die but departs together with son—Paul and Clovis reunited; recorrected in that painter Paul now turns the tables and leaves son Clovis, as father Clovis had died leaving painter son Paul. During the course of his life the pattern was to be repeated: he had five more children with young girls between 13 and 17, only to abandon them either when they were well along in pregnancy or had recently given birth.

To continue this saga, there are indications that mother's death, like father's, may also have been elaborated in the context of death and rebirth symbolism both in reliving and in art. Gauguin had been 19 when his mother died. As Gedo (1989) points out, the artist may have commemorated her death at ten-year intervals thereafter with major enactments: when a daughter was born near the tenth anniversary of mother's death she was named Aline, after his mother; on the twentieth anniversary of mother's death, he had arranged to be on the Caribbean island of Martinique.

Gauguin was already in Tahiti around the thirtieth anniversary of mother Aline's death when he was informed that his 20-year-old daughter Aline had died on January 19, 1897. He suffered a major depression and provoked the final end of correspondence with his wife and their children. Between October 10 and October 12 of that year he suffered a series of heart attacks. He decided to commit suicide; then, opting for life, changed his mind on October 15, 1897. In terms of the clinical fact that unconscious death and rebirth fantasies may often seize upon the nine-month interval of gestation as a biologically determined temporal framework within which to express themselves (Rose, 1962, 1969, 1972), it is striking to observe that Gauguin's heart attacks as well as his decisions for death and for life took place in the last week of the ninth month after his daughter died.

About six weeks later Gauguin had another heart attack but instead of entering the hospital he began his large "testament" painting, *Where Do We Come From? What Are We? Where Are We Going?* Apparently either his work did not succeed in relieving his depression or else it recurred, because by the end of the month—it was also the end of the year, December 30, 1897—he was suicidal again. He went into the mountains and tried to destroy himself with arsenic but only made himself ill. Nine months later he impregnated his 16-year-old *vahine*; this was to be a son, Emile, the same name as his first child, born twenty-five years earlier.

Turning now to some death and rebirth symbolism in Gauguin's art, an 1889 painting entitled *Life and Death* depicts the forces of life and death embodied in the form of two female nudes. One derives from a Peruvian mummy that Gauguin had seen in the Musée de l 'Homme in Paris— in fetal position, feet crossed, legs and arms drawn inward, head tilted. In the painting the skeleton is replaced with a new image of a bather in the crouched mummy's position. She also appears in other paintings of the period, notably the *Breton Eve*.

The following year the Eve theme is rearranged in *Eve Exotique*, the forerunner of many Tahitian Eves to follow. The body of the female nude now comes from the Buddhist Borobudur temple reliefs in Java. Her surroundings are taken from the painter's memories of Martinique. Most importantly, her face comes from a photograph of the artist's mother. What began as death, in the form of a Peruvian mummy, has been reversed: first transformed into a primal mother, Eve, and then reborn in Polynesia as his own mother as a young island girl. That it had special meaning for Gauguin is suggested by the fact that he did not sign or date this painting, or ever put it up for sale.

These various nine-month sequences and memorial enactments of death and rebirth suggest a context for the androgynous themes in Gauguin's *oeuvre*. As one can readily demonstrate, these had always been present from the earliest to his latest works. His first frankly symbolic creation was a carved jewel box on the inside of which he carved an ambiguously sexed youth in the position of a mummy. And for a grave marker, Gauguin chose his ceramic sculpture of the mythic Polynesian god of Death, *Oviri*. Combining the head of a mummy with the body of a Javanese goddess of fertility, and crushing a wolf under her feet while clasping a wolf cub to her side, Gauguin referred to it as *La Tueuse, The Murderess*. Elsewhere he related it to Balzac's novel *Seraphita*, in which the hero is androgynous.

Between 1888 and 1889 in Brittany, he did four male nudes. *Young Breton Bather* is a side-view drawing of a young male, his genital clearly depicted in profile. The painting, *Young Bretons Bathing*, depicts a pair of male nudes with their backs to each other, one standing and the other seated, his genital concealed. In *Children Wrestling* (1888, Catalogue W. 273), the boys are now in intimate contact but wearing shorts. The last one, *Nude Breton Boy* (1889, Catalogue W. 339), shows a boy lying on his back in a position described as looking "both unwilling and uncomfortable. . . . Oddly, Gauguin has refused to paint the boy's genitals" (Brettel, Cachin, Freches-Thory, and Stuckey, 1988, p. 151). Later that same year, Gauguin painted *Yellow Christ* (K. 327) showing Christ as weak and unmasculine.

In Brittany he had admired the women who were as robust and husky as men, carried heavy loads, and ran the farms. Arriving in Tahiti in 1891 he now marveled that "the difference between the sexes is less accentuated than in our climates" and that "there is something virile in the women and something feminine in the men" (Gauguin, 1919, pp. 19–20). He painted *Man with an Ax* (1891, W. 430), portraying a somewhat androgynous Tahitian, and for a decade thereafter rarely depicted another Tahitian man.

His artistic output in Tahiti concentrated on children, animals, and mythic women, sometimes monumental and threatening. Potiphar's wife, for example, done at the end of his career, portrays her attacking a recoiling Joseph. Several female nudes have an ambiguous, almost androgynous, quality. This is especially true for *Pape Moe* (*Mysterious Water*, 1893, Catalogue W. 498). It is based on a photograph of a Tahitian *man* drinking water from a waterfall in a grotto. The woman in the painting clearly retains the man's muscularity.

Let us place ourselves now at a particular time and place

in Gauguin's life: after several years in Tahiti, he is back in Paris (with his Javanese mistress), living in a flat below that of a young musician friend, William Molard. It is the winter of 1893–1894. Gauguin is 46 years of age (he will die just before turning 55). He is standing in front of a blank new canvas.

Recalling our image of the creative system as a partially opaque, two-way mirror, let us suppose that, whatever conscious notions he may have about what he wishes to make happen on the canvas, less conscious currents of feeling-thought also influence what takes shape on the canvas. For Gauguin believes in "dreaming" while fully awake before nature and now before the canvas, letting the "dreams" suggest the painting and the translation of the feeling into visual terms. "Art is an abstraction; derive this abstraction from nature while dreaming before it" (quoted by Goldwater, 1983, p. 38).

This particular canvas is going to be a self-portrait entitled *Self-Portrait with Hat* (1893–1894). The artist carefully arranges his scene in front of an actual mirror. This we do know because one of his most significant paintings from the South Seas takes shape in the background of the self-portrait with the image reversed. It is in a bright yellow frame and is one of the strongest points in the picture, the other being the look in the vivid green of the model's eye (Brettell et al., 1988, p. 312).

Moving into the self-portrait, what is the painting Gauguin has chosen to depict in the background? It is *Manao Tupapau* (*Spirit of the Dead Watching*, late 1892). It is considered to "represent a brilliant resume of all the formal and theoretical progress he had made since his arrival in the South Seas" (Brettell et al., 1988, pp. 279, 280–282).

Gauguin took the idea for the painting from a recent memory, serving as a kind of day residue. He had arrived

Paul Gauguin: *Self-Portrait with Hat* (1893–1894). Paris, Musée d'Orsay

Paul Gauguin: *The Spirit of the Dead Watching*, 1892, oil on burlap mounted on canvas, 28½ × 36⅜ inches. Albright-Knox Art Gallery, Buffalo, New York. A. Conger Goodyear Collection, 1965.

home in his native village after midnight and saw his teen-age vahine, Tehura, lying motionless, naked, belly down on the bed, staring up at him from a surrounding mass of colors: on a yellow blanket over a blue sarong against a violet background.

A number of elements impacted immediately: visual, emotional, and narrative—probably in that order. He was struck by her loveliness and beauty. "And, in the *half-shadow*, which no doubt seethed with dangerous apparitions and *ambiguous shapes* . . . [and in] the phosphorescent light [that] poured from her staring eyes . . . wide with fear . . . she seemed not to know who I was. For a moment *I too felt a strange uncertainty*. Tehura's dread was contagious" (from *Noa Noa* [1919], quoted by Brettell et al., 1988, p. 280; emphasis added). He began to wonder (narrative element) if she took him for one of those legendary specters, the *Tupapaus*, or spirits of the dead, that haunt the dreams of her people?

When this teeming perception was later worked over in the light of his artist-memory, it tapped into two art histori-cal sources to become transformed into his own conception, the *Manao tupapau*. The year before, at the Luxembourg Museum, Gauguin had copied Manet's *Olympia* (1863). That model's unabashed frontal nudity, as she stares almost bra-zenly out at the viewer from her reclining posture while waited on by her black maidservant, was intended to be a right-in-your-face aimed at Parisian academia. It is consid-ered to be one source for Gauguin's *Manao tupapau*, earn-ing it the title of "the Olympia of Tahiti."

Evidently, Gauguin transformed Manet's black maid servant into a brooding Spirit of Death, that model's frank gaze into Tehura's fearfulness, and by turning her onto her belly to conform with the memory of Tehura, transformed a picture of frontal female nudity into one of *ambiguous* gender—in the "half-shadow" of Gauguin's own gender "uncertainty."

Supporting this view of the androgynous character of Gauguin's *Manao tupapau* is the second art historical source of the painting: "an engraving by the neo-classic Dutch painter Humbert de Superville representing a reclining *youth* haunted by a specter with a death's head" (Brettell et al., 1988, p. 281; emphasis added).

As for the canvas that serves as our two-way mirror, *Self-portrait with Hat*, with the (androgynous) *Manao tupapau* in the background, on the *other* side of the canvas is *another* picture. We have no way of knowing which painting came first. It is a full-face portrait of his friend upstairs, William Molard. Before jumping to conclusions about the sexual nature of Gauguin's interest in Molard, however, we must note that Molard also happened to have a daughter, Judith. Like Tehura, the model for *Manao tupapau*, and all his other mistresses, including his current "Javanaise," Judith was a teenager and "frequently played the daughter of the house for Gauguin when he entertained his artistic and literary friends. . . . At all events, he gave Molard this two-sided canvas as a sign of his friendship and gratitude" (Brettell et al., 1988, p. 312).

Summarizing this two-sided canvas, we have a portrait of a man on either side, "between" which we may infer a kind of mental *montage* of male, female, and androgynous nudes— reflecting various self-images.

By August of 1899, about five years later and back in Tahiti, Gauguin more or less stopped painting. Like his father, he now turned to journalism. He entered fully into the political life of the colonial government of Tahiti as writer, editor, and publisher. Given the fact that his political style was combative and bristling—perhaps further "released" by a tertiary syphilitic process—it is interesting that

Manet: *Olympia* (1863). Paris, Musée d'Orsay

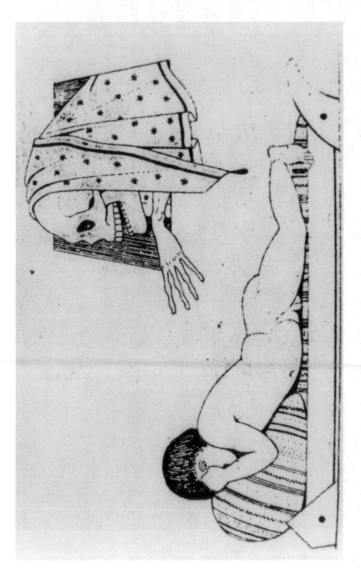

de Superville: *Allegory* (1801), etching. Pkentenkabinet Der Rijksuniver-sitet, Leiden

Paul Gauguin: *Portrait of William Molard.* Paris, Musée d'Orsay

he again began to paint males, but of a soft and effeminate quality. *Riders* (1901, Catalogue W. 597)—aside from some self-portraits, his first painting in five years dealing exclusively with males—shows a hooded figure on a white horse, a Polynesian *tupapau* or "spirit of the dead" who leads a young man across a stream to a mythic land beyond death.

Then, in 1902, "he seems to have become almost obsessed with ambiguous male sexuality" (Brettell et al., 1988, p. 481). Without any clear precedent from his earlier work, he painted a series of works that represent effeminate men with long hair. This was clearly a *mahu*, a type of effeminate man well known and accepted in Polynesian society as one raised from childhood as a woman. The first one was *Marquesan Man in a Red Cape* (W. 616), followed by *Bathers* (W. 618) and *The Lovers* (W. 614). In the same year he did a gouache, *Bather* (F. 133). The graceful contours of a figure sitting on a rock in the middle of a stream indicate that this is a woman. But the short hair turns the figure into an androgyne. *Riders on the Beach* (W. 620) shows a *mahu* pair conversing. One, astride a horse, is long-haired and wearing a woman's white shift. Two colorfully costumed *tupapau* are on gray-white horses as figures of death.

Gauguin's (Neoplatonic) vision of a perfect person was one who transcended gender—a union of male and female complete in a paradisal tropical garden of nature. When he first arrived in Tahiti, the islanders, surprised by his long hair, nicknamed him taata-vahine, man/woman. He wrote, "I was *reborn*; or rather another man, purer and stronger, *came to life within me*" (Gauguin, 1919, p. 22; emphasis added). Apparently, in this paradisal world, he had succeeded in transcending gender and achieving his own ideal—he felt reborn an androgyne!

How are we to understand the inner workings of this rebirth and transformation? More generally, how can we approach the larger question of the relationship, if any, between art and androgyny? A working frame of reference might include the following possibilities, bearing in mind that in the case of any particular artist various combinations and relative strengths might be found to exist.

First, there may be no relationship per se between art and androgyny. Art might reflect various latent or overt elements of the artist's nature, and in any given instance the androgynous component might not be sufficiently significant or discernible in the present.

Related to this would be the idea that the only connection between androgyny and art might be after the fact. That is to say, androgynous elements might not play a significant role at the source of art. Rather, art could be put to some secondarily adaptive or defensive purpose. For example, art might serve as a substitute for emotional relatedness in general (e.g., Edvard Munch), including hetero- or homosexual relationships. Another example, just as art may be used fetishistically in primitive societies to provide magical protection against projected fears, it can also be used as a private fetish to bolster ego boundaries weakened by psychopathology, including body-image boundaries and confused gender identities. Or, to rationalize personal failings: for example, in order to compensate for his known propensity to lie, exploit, and deceive, Gauguin could point to his art technique that emphasized flat planes which he considered "honest." He said he avoided vague outlines because they permitted "subterfuge" and "deceit."

The data of this chapter might warrant a number of different scenarios. Forced to grow up without a father, Gauguin identified with his mother as well as his dead father, and as I have sketched out, enacted both identifications in the form of repeated separations and reunions, symbolized as deaths and rebirths. As a result of the double identification, however, he had a weakly defined gender identity. His art was a creative outlet for the feminine aspect of his identification—a sublimation of the female reproductive capacity. However, he had to compensate for the repressed feminine aspects by setting himself many *macho* tasks including the compulsion to consume young girls. Finally, weakened by disease, the homoerotic component emerged in the form of the pronounced androgynous theme of his late work and, by his own account (Gauguin, 1919, p. 20), in a single outburst of homosexual infatuation which he succeeded in controlling.

Another formulation bases itself upon the importance of the experience of parental deadness—either through actual death or the emotional deadness of depression. Gauguin's father, as we know, died when Paul was an infant of 17 months. His mother was described (by George Sand) at 19 as sad and grieving even before she was widowed at 22.

The experience of such actual or emotional parental deadness can have a number of significant consequences. It can lead to premature disillusionment, unconscious identification with the dead or emotionally dead parent, and inner states of emptiness and loss of meaning (Green, 1986). The sense of inner deadness may also lead clinically to feeling full of hatred, or needing to compensate by a "lust for life" and search for excitement. In terms of homosexual dynamics it can lead to the wish to merge with a partner of the same sex to reinfuse one's own gender identity with a sense of aliveness; or defend against such a homoerotic choice through compulsive heterosexuality.

This brings us to an alternative to the one-sided view that art is to be understood psychodynamically as a creative outlet for identification with female reproductivity. Creativity draws on the fullest possible sense of *wholeness* of the individual including his or her maleness *and* female-ness. Coleridge remarked that "a great mind must be an-drogynous," something which apparently had been intu-ited since ancient times. The *Tao Te Ching*, for example, speaks of the importance of knowing the masculine yet keeping to the feminine, in order to "become a channel drawing all the world towards it" (Lao Tze [c. 600 b.c., p. xxviii], quoted by Milner [1973]).

Translating this into a more modern if less poetic idiom, one might say that fresh vision, whether in the analytic pro-cess or in the major forms of creativity, involves a cyclical rhythm. There is a "letting-down" and reimposition of or-der: an alternating suspension of daily logic and the I/Not-I split, a wide-angle active attentiveness to the whole gamut of bodily and mental impressions as they are allowed to hap-pen; and an active, sharp-focused reshaping of the malleable material that presents itself. This oscillating rhythm can be thought of as an interplay of knowledge and imagination, or more technically as secondary and primary processes (Rose, 1980, 1987). Each side of the rhythm is inherently *active* in its own characteristic way, and each needs the other to ensure psychic fertility. This figure of speech is used de-liberately in order to indicate that the rhythm seems to lend itself readily to being symbolized (as in the *Tao Te Ching*) as male and female. This becomes clinically significant when such sexualization takes place unconsciously and be-comes invested with *passive* meanings, for this often stimu-lates homosexual and castration anxieties and leads to cre-ative inhibition.

Let us place this sense of male–female wholeness—or biphasic rhythm of active wide-angle receptivity and ac-tive sharp-focused reshaping of the data of consciousness—into a developmental frame of reference. It is based on the image of an undifferentiated matrix of child and parent—

the preoedipal primal unity that precedes separateness and knowledge of gender. Such a phallic mother imago can be a healthy wellspring of activity and creativity in both sexes.

We cannot know whether Gauguin, by virtue of his creative gift, knew how to draw upon this source within himself; or to what extent the dual identification with his depressed mother and the idea of his dead father constituted a threat of inner deadness that forced him to fall back on these early resources within himself. We may suspect that the threat of inner deadness played a role in stimulating compensatory fantasies of rebirth; that these in turn drew upon the undifferentiated, androgynous matrix within himself and tapped into the biological urge to be productive.

Identification with the early image of the parent who has and can do everything, in addition to being a source of activity and creativity for both sexes, may also be a source of narcissistic and hermaphroditic omnipotence that carries its own neurotic potential. Gauguin could be his own father and mother, self-sufficient, invulnerable even to death. Needing no one and being able to do everything himself, he could boast of having run away as a child and having raped a little girl, he could be a noble savage without any need for a fatherland, he could claim credit for the ideas of others (Emile Bernard's synthetism), and for having been a teacher to van Gogh.

He could also flail against decadent conventions, flaunt his appetite for young girls, exploit and fall out with male colleagues, and engage in polemics against the establishment. The anxious counterphobic core of his sexual exhibitionism and pugnacious autonomy could well elude conscious awareness; for example, it was only after he reached his mother's age at her death (42) that he turned from adult women to pedophilia (Gedo, 1989). Or, there was his un-awareness that it was his own aggressive voraciousness that he feared and projected onto adult women.

Above all, such immunity to limitations of all kinds would be consistent with an unconscious belief in his own actual immortality—as, of course, he did succeed in achieving for his name and his art—by virtue of his own uncommon genius rather than his not uncommon omnipotent androgyny.

Turning from the commonality shared by Gauguin's mind with that of many others, and turning to his special genius, what might be said of his art as *art*? In a notebook written for his daughter, Gauguin offered two levels of "explana-tion" of his paintings "for those who always have to know the whys and the wherefores" (quoted in Brettell et al., 1988, p. 281). These are: the level of narrative content, which he referred to as "the literary part" and the formal aspects, which he sometimes referred to as "the poem" or, more usually, the "musical part."

Regarding the *Manao tupapau*, for example, on a narra-tive level it is "simply a study of a Polynesian nude" with some kind of a story behind it; whereas, in its purely visual, plastic, or formal aspects it is "harmony . . . sounding on the eye . . . Undulating horizontal lines—harmonies in orange and blue linked by yellows and violets, from which they derive. The light and the greenish sparks" (quoted by Bret-tell et al., 1988, p. 281).

In terms of a possible "story" for the painting, he had wondered: "What would a young native girl be doing in that daring and naked position: preparing for love, or sleeping, after the act of love?" He had rejected such a content for his picture as indecent and he did not want that. The only possible thing was fear. Of what? Accord-ing to Tahitian beliefs, either she thinks of the ghost or the ghost thinks of her. He intuited her belief in a symbolic linkage between herself, a living girl, with the spirit of Death.

The "musical" or formal aspect of painting seems clearly to be of greater importance for Gauguin, and he kept alluding to music as the standard to strive for. Thus: "Painting should seek suggestion more than description, as indeed, music does" (letter to De Manfried [1901], quoted by Goldwater [1983, pp. 40–42]). Again:

> These repetitions of tone, in monotone chords (in the musical sense of color), . . . analogous to Oriental chants, sung in a shrill voice and accompanied by resonant notes. . . . Beethoven frequently used this. . . . Thinking about what I say, look closely at Cimabue. Think also about the musical part to be played in modern painting *from now on.* Color, which is vibration as well as music, attaining . . . nature['s] . . . interior force" [letter to Fontainas, March 1899; quoted by Brettell et al., 1988, p. 393n; emphasis added].

Read "abstract" for "musical." This is where the level of significance is to be found. This is the insight that illuminated Gauguin's career, anticipating much that is basic to all modern art: all art is an abstraction. The sense of a picture lies not in its title or its subject, but in its visual elements; its lasting value is related only indirectly to representation or content. The arrangement of its lines, shapes, and colors are abstract forms that, lacking material being, yet have the power to evoke feelings. When we approach Gauguin's canvases from our side of the two-way looking-glass, we pass through our own intermediate mix of subject and object into this realm of the abstract that transcends the personal.

Breton had asked, "If art is a window, the question is, on what?"

On outside and inside, one ventures to answer. Witnessing self *and* other, other *in* self, the world of the abstract beyond both—as feelings resonate to forms.

But Magritte was right: the danger always is that centering for too long on the question, What does it MEAN? and the *words . . . words . . . words* with which to try to answer takes us further from art as "witness" to feelingful experience.

4

ART AND AFFECT:
MUSIC INSIDE/OUT
AND VICE VERSA

> *What is the aim of philosophy? To show
> the fly the way out of the fly-bottle.*
> —Wittgenstein (1953)

Gauguin had noted: "Color, . . . like music, is vibration."
Apparently with that as sufficient license, he then conflated
painting with music and predicted the significance of "the
musical part to be played in modern painting *from now on*"
(letter to Fontainas, March 1899, quoted by Brettell, Cachin,
Freches-Thory, and Stuckey [1988, p. 393n]).

Certainly not one to value reason over emotion, he might
even have subscribed to the saying that logic is a systematic
way of arriving at the *wrong* conclusion with confidence.
His equating of music with painting thus needs, rather, to
be placed in the poetic–philosophical perspective of his
time.

It was a deeply felt metaphor in the context of French
Symbolism, which emphasized the importance of nuance
and ambiguity, rather than sharp realistic boundaries. In

that it insisted on the reality of the *imagination*, it may be considered an outgrowth of romanticism. Imagination propels one beyond prosaic reasonableness into a less tangible world of emotions, dreams, suggestions, and impressions where there is no rigid separation of the self from the nonself. Symbolists understood that the task of exploring the (Platonic) unity underlying the multiplicity of appearances and, conversely, the multiplicity of meanings latent within the unitary symbol is more the task of poetic intuition and imagination than of logic (Peyre, 1974).

Symbolism was one of the most fruitful movements of artistic and literary life in France toward the end of the nineteenth century—a time and place, let it be noted, when psychoanalysis was beginning to germinate in the mind of the young Freud listening spellbound to the cosmopolitan Charcot lecturing on hypnosis.

It was in that same period that Walter Pater wrote: "All art constantly aspires to the condition of music" (1873, p. 16). This was a symbolist view very much in the air of that time—in the same spirit, for example, as Verlaine, who voiced an impassioned cry for the primacy of music in poetry. For Gauguin this emphasis on music meant nothing less than creating an art that rescued the emotional core of perception from the banality of realistic dailiness—an art that conveyed "emotion . . . at the most intimate part of the soul" (Gauguin, 1974, p. 131).

The danger, of course, is that intuitive emotional values—unrestrained—feed upon themselves and turn into the sheer wildness of extreme subjectivism and unintelligibility. The enthronement of nonrationalism can stretch the boundaries between inside and outside to the point of dissolving the self. (In our time, some of the extreme manifestations of modern malaise reflected in modernism and postmodernism may be related to the hyperreflexivity, solipsistic gran-

deur, and abject metaphysical terror of an unfolding schizophrenic process (Sass, 1992).

Most of the French symbolists did, indeed, fall into oblivion. The poetry of Mallarmé survived but, haunted like
later existentialists with the idea of nothingness, he seemed
to disdain cognitive intelligibility altogether. Instead of at-
tempting to reconstruct his poetry's hallucinatory visions
and the "meaning" of the language, a reader's creative participation is better enlisted in the flow of the music and the
currents of affect that rise within one to meet it.

Nevertheless, despite the symbolist equating of music
with visual art and poetry, one cannot obliterate that one
listens to music differently from the way one *views* painting.
Art and music may both be likened to windows for redis-
covering the outside, revealing in turn the inside (cf. Chapter 3), transforming the terms of perception—the way we
see and hear. It is undoubtedly true, too, that each experience changes in the course of time as one revisits a loved
painting or hears a new performance of familiar music, and
the memory traces of the past reblend into the present. But,
the quality of hearing's interiority differs markedly from
seeing's distance—with some degree of overlap allowed for
those rare circumstances where color seems to perfuse the
air one breathes (the greenness of the Dordogne area of
France, the blueness of Istanbul's Blue Mosque).

Where *is* the music? In a person's head? The musical
structure? The tones themselves? Music and affective response interpenetrate as one. We hear it best eyes closed;
better still, lying down. Relating through one's body, its
pulse, moving with its directionality like a swimmer in the
current, yet not of it.

Not so with vision. We awaken *to* it, reenter *its* domain.
Night falls—*it* leaves.

Music never left. We wake to it, already there. Only its

source—inside, outside?—waiting to be discriminated, located objectively, reembodied. Does it rejoin us, or we it? Its motion to our e-motion? (cf. Spitz, 1991)

The task of this and the following chapters is to recruit some of the strands of psychoanalytic thought through which we may freshly attempt to relate art and affect. To anticipate the issue, we will hold that affect resides in the *congruence* of formal dynamic patterns of tension and release between inside and outside, ego and art, joining in an interplay of apparent attunement with emotional resonances.

Art and culture have been said to occupy a kind of "intermediate area" characterized by a "*mixture* of external and internal reality" (Riviere, 1936, p. 399; Winnicott, 1953). The emotional resonances between therapist and patient may also be thought of as occupying such an intermediate area, and the value of that experience lies largely in monitoring and exploring the fluctuations that take place therein. Indeed, it is only the familiarity of working clinically within this microframe of reference that emboldens one to face up to the fact that the focus of our interest, the intermediate area between ego and reality, is the traditional province of philosophy and religion.

The traditional religious view is that an ordered, coherent, and harmonious reality, partially discoverable by the mind, reflects "a divine exemplar" (sermons preached to the Pope in the Sistine Chapel and in Saint Peter's basilica between 1450 and 1521 [O'Malley, 1979, quoted by Gay, 1992, p. 6]). An ancient proverb: he who sings well prays *twice*. (For this reference I am indebted to a correspondent, Professor M. J. Tucker, who owes it to Father Val Welker.) Theology, says Luther, begins where music leads to.

For Freud (who had little taste for music or theology), qualitative experiences are *subjective illusions*. They come about because of the infant's need to evolve slowly from primary narcissism in order to survive and respond to the claims of others. The way they come about is through the ego working over the bare "quantities" of sense data impinging on the organism from the outside world. Quantities are "in" the world, providing objective scientific facts; they are in perpetual motion, obeying immutable laws of the physical universe. Qualities, on the other hand, exist only in the mind of the individual as subjective *values*. They are constructed out of the organism's current *libidinal state*.

In point of fact, probably most practicing analysts no longer choose sides between subjective "qualities" and objective "quantities." The controversy between Freud and Ferenczi is moot: Ferenczi who insisted that the patient must come to terms with his historical traumas; Freud who was preoccupied with the impact of the patient's own fantasies on the so-called traumas. Obviously these complementary emphases involve an interweaving of new experiences and a reinterpretation of the past in an *open system*. Psychic reality is constantly changing in response to new meanings in intercourse with reality and the incessant pressure to engage others in our desires (Kirshner, 1993).

However, to the extent that the aforementioned beliefs form the basis for Freud's theory of art, going back in his thought as far as the "Project" (1895), all subsequent psychoanalytic attempts to fill the gap between the deep origins and the surface qualities of experience are rendered equally deficient, in the opinion of a contemporary critic (Gay, 1992): "distance from the drives," neutralization or desexualization, identification and displacement, narcissistic and object libido, as well as attempts by linguistic metapsychology, phenomenology, and structuralism. The same holds for later attempts to refine sublimation into an achievement whereby the ego uses its archaic heritage of fantasy to solve old problems in a new way.

The basis for this judgment is that Freud's philosophical commitment to the distinction between real, objective quantities and illusional, subjective qualities makes the sensuous surface of things—which is, after all, the proper focus of aesthetic interest—a mystery. Neither creator nor audience can have direct knowledge of the underlying internal process.

There is no denying, it seems to me, that too exclusive a focus on unconscious dynamics and regression short-changes the multifariousness of external reality and thus undercuts the value of traditional psychoanalytic aesthetics. But are there no paths leading from within psychoanalysis—meaning, without undue sacrifice of psychoanalysis itself—to a fuller appreciation of the sensuous surfaces of experience, the appropriate focus of aesthetic interest?

Freud did hold that the mental apparatus must have in its structure some accurate means of innately attending to reality despite being played upon by (correctable) unconscious fantasies. Rapaport (1957) noted that ego structures require sensory nutriment from the environment to maintain their integrity against drive pressures, and also depend on objects in the environment as well as drives in order not to become enslaved to stimuli in the environment.

Still better suited to our purpose is Hartmann's (1956) hypothesis that the perceptual system (among others) constitutes an inborn apparatus of primary autonomy *pretuned* to external reality. He wrote: "The child is born with a certain degree of preadaptiveness; . . . the apparatus of perception . . . which help[s] us to deal with reality [is], in a primitive form, already present at birth; later . . . will mature and develop in constant reaction, of course, with experience" (p. 246).

If we return to the expressive quality of perception and assume that this is the particular aspect of perception's primary autonomy that is pretuned to the *dynamic qualities* of reality—meaning, tension, and release—I suggest that this provides a theoretical bridge into the intermediate area of mixed external and internal reality—the domain of culture and art.

We turn now to a brief historical overview of attempts to deal with the meaning of music by variably weighing its rootedness in world or mind (Neubauer, 1986). We will note a steady trend toward interiorizing its significance in the mind of the listener, while retaining its attachments to the external world—a historical correlative of an intermediate phenomenon.

Music has historically been considered to be related to the external world of nature and of the cosmic order. As for the first, the theory of mimesis held that music embodied representational meanings standing for external objects or events (bird whistles). Pythagoreanism and other mathematical approaches to music connected it to the natural cosmic order. These views start from the observation that the frequency ratios of the octave and intervals of the fifth and the fourth are 1:2, 2:3, and 3:4, respectively. Musical harmony thus expressed the balance of things: movements of the planets, elements, humors of the body, soul, and soma, the body politic. Meaning is encoded in the relationship between music, mathematics, and harmonics. This cosmic scope marked it as being a divine gift.

In Monteverdi's time (1567–1643), a rhetorical theory placed language at the center of music's expressiveness. His operas imitated aspects of language. Composers used means comparable to the classical oratory of Cicero and Aristotle to control and direct the audience's feelings.

Less precise than these rhetorical principles were the affect theories of music that flourished in the eighteenth century. They aimed at short-circuiting language by correlating emotions with aspects of sound: keys, intervals, meters, instruments. Music was meant to represent and arouse affects.

Affect theories of music were loose and unsystematic. Descartes (1596–1650) had already noted that different stimuli could arouse the same emotion, and the same stimulus could lead to different emotions. He believed that the emotional response depended on the ideas and memories of the listener—a strikingly modern notion!

A century later, Diderot (1713–1784) also placed the meaning of music in the mind of the listener who endows music with personal meanings. Anticipating Kant, he held that the listener constructs meanings that are generated by the music.

Kant (1724–1804) taught that art brought about a balanced and free play of mental powers and, in so doing, engenders in the receiver's mind more than inheres in art itself. It follows that the recipient's mind makes a creative contribution to the working of art. This emphatically takes art out of the cosmic (Pythagorean) order and places it in relation to an internal order in the minds of both artist and recipient.

What is the internal order? Art invites an intuitive perception of an internal organization between parts and whole by way of such principles as symmetry, contrast, repetition, and rhythm rather than determinate meanings and content. The dichotomy of form and content dissolves: content is embodied in form, as anatomy embodies physiology. Structure carries function; function expresses structure.

Herder (1744–1803) shifted Kant's emphasis from the observer cultivating a disinterested contemplation of art to the notion that the order of art *evolves*, and that this depends on the receiver's sympathetic temperamental *resonance*. This opens the door further to the possibility that aesthetic experience may change in the course of time and generations, die, or indeed, experience renascence, thus transcending a biological curve.

This returns us to the external pole of a transcendent order. Unlike Pythagoreanism, however, and the music of the spheres in extrahuman outer space, the return has come about through an internal journey and "metabolized" over time through human minds resonating to the dynamic shapes of music. Neither subjective passion alone, nor objective rationality, music represents a subjective objectivity demanding emotional intensity *and* sober detachment (E. T. A. Hoffmann, 1776–1822).

Within our own century, this evolution of thinking about music has been eloquently expressed by Susan Langer (1953): art represents a subjectification of outward forms and an objectification of inner feelings. A related view, more recently: "Music is . . . a vehicle of passion . . . which expresses inwardness but also intimates, by means of mathematics, a higher order" (Neubauer, 1986, p. 200); in our own terms, a suitable cultural representative of Winnicott's intermediate area of ego-reality.

Back again to the question of the *qualities* of reality: are they inherent in reality, "out there," whether or not ascribable to divinity, or in the mind of the recipient, whether or not ascribable to libidinal states? Our brief account of the evolution of thinking about music speaks for a rootedness on both sides but with the historical direction being toward the organizing influence of internal states of mind.

However, the debate continues. Instead of asking, "How are we to understand the phenomenon of music?" Victor Zuckerkandl turned the question around to, "Given the phenomenon of music, what does this say about the world?" —and came down on the side of the qualities inherent in music itself. (I am grateful to Maria Bergmann and Irma Rogell for having brought his books [1956, 1973] to my attention.) I will extract from his discourse what is relevant to the present purpose.

While Langer holds that tonal patterns are the nondiscursive symbols of the "inner life" or "morphology of feeling" of a psyche, Zuckerkandl (1973) boldly places the locus of significance of musical tones in "the tone's own dynamic quality" (p. 154). "Tones are not primarily something external related to some inner life; the relationship between external and internal is wholly embedded in the tone itself" (p. 153). Thus, in a musical view of the universe we encounter a purely dynamic, nonphysical element of nature, attained not through religious revelation but through sense perception and observation.

The key to hearing music, in contrast to listening to mere acoustic sounds, involves discovering forces that are active in tones and tonal systems. It is the reality of these forces that makes music possible—perhaps even irrespective of the quality of the particular work. These forces endow tones with dynamic qualities: tension, direction, motion. In dynamic quality we hear what the tone strives for, perceived directly as forces in action. It is not a matter of ratios of pitch and duration; these are merely acoustical, and what is an acoustically wrong tone can be musically right if in accordance with the sense of the movement. Ordered tonal motion may be heard not only in melodic line but harmonically in chords as interpenetrating tones that relate to each other dynamically while each also remains separate.

Zuckerkandl (1973) is at his best in explicating the scale as a dynamic field of forces.

> Motion along the scale is not a constant rise in relation to pitch but a rise *and* fall in relation to tonal forces, a departure from

... and approach to ... [Furthermore] the center of the dynamic field is not present merely in one place but is reproduced in every new octave. ... Going away from the center of force, we immediately find ourselves going toward ... its repetition at the next octave. It has anticipated the issue, it is always ahead of the motion; always we have before us what we have left behind us. ... As infallibly as, in our breathing, every expiration is a departure from a previous inspiration and at the same time an approach to the next inspiration. ... The world of tone ... [has] the form of the wave ... pulse ... respiration [p. 104].

This explication of the musical scale is essentially in the spirit of Bergsonian "duration": living, physiological time, the order of biology. Just as in living processes, the immaterial dynamic forces embodied in musical tones have to do with the tendency to move from unbalance to balance, and the relations between *tension and release*. The same law governing living processes becomes audible in ordered tonal motion: "every step, as it is being made is free; once made, it is necessary. Freedom in prospect, necessity in retrospect" (Zuckerkandl, 1973, p. 146). (This accords with common clinical experience in reconstructing a life history; in hindsight what actually happened convincingly appears to have been psychodynamically determined—but not why at the time something else did not occur.)

Is there a place for verbal meanings or content in the world of music? This question, Zuckerkandl holds, has no application because it comes from the realm of verbal language which makes distinctions as to things, subjects, and objects. In contrast, "tones build a bridge over the boundaries between subjectivity and objectivity which words spell out" (1973, p. 72). "[R]unning [not] between self and world, but ... through both ... bring[ing] to expression the mode of existence of the world that is of the same nature as ... my psyche . . ." (Zuckerkandl, 1956, p. 370). "Tones hold up for our perception, as real, a dimension of the world that transcends all individual distinctions of things and therefore all verbal language" (p. 372).

This is a way of stating that words, unless used as vehicles of art, are incommensurable with art.

These various references—relating music to breathing, living, physiological time, or repeated movement from unbalance to balance, or a sense of free anticipation followed by an experience of inevitability after the fact—direct our attention to actual musical *performance*. Why does one live performance feel "right" and another "wrong"—totally apart, needless to say, from technical proficiency?

And what do a conductor's movements and choreography contribute to an audience's experience? Do they not concentrate the kinetic gestures inherent in the music? Perhaps this acts as a model to help one identify and feel in one's body the music from within—its vibration, touch, pulse, direction—as one's own, inseparable from affect.

The dynamic buildup and release of tensions in musical structure is perhaps "the essential factor conveying the sensation of movement, of motion." Motion, in turn, may well be "the key to the pragmatic decisions that continually beset performers and composers in pursuing their goal of controlled affective statement" (Epstein, in press). And since ritards and accelerations are among the most common musical devices for controlling "motion" and thus affect, in order to study this, samples of ritards and accelerations that were judged to be aesthetically "good" or "bad" were selected from a group of recorded musical performances (Epstein, 1995).

Plotting the rate of ritard or acceleration of the "good" performances onto a graph yielded results that conformed remarkably (94 to 97%) to a geometric cubic curve. The "bad" performances were largely off the curve to either side.

Since a cubic curve also describes the way the nervous system processes periodicity and other aspects of timing tendencies, the "good" aesthetic curve is apparently congruent with basic neurophysiological propensities. These, in turn, may "serve as something of a timing template against which we inevitably compare the actual curve being performed" (Epstein, 1993, p. 121). The degree to which the performance matches the underlying neurophysiological timing propensity could thus provide an organic basis for the "good" aesthetic experience.

This paradigm would assign one source of the "good" aesthetic experience to the innate tendency of the nervous system to process time via equal quanta. Moreover, this could extend beyond accelerations and ritards to include all aspects of *timing* in music. According to Roger Sessions, the *external*, musical elements of timing in music are the ones that "reproduce . . . all . . . the fine shades of dynamic variation of our *inner* life" (Cone, 1979, p. 19).

The close correspondence between judgments of aesthetically "good" performances of accelerations or ritards and the attributes of a cubic curve need not locate qualities of experience either "in" the world or "in" the mind and imparted "to" the world by the mind. Rather, the degree of *congruence* between timing in the external world and in one's own organic structure appears to be reflected in both performer's and listener's sense of the "rightness" or "wrongness" of a musical experience.

May we work from this statement to a more general one relating the *qualities* of experience to *congruence*? We might begin by proposing that the congruence between "inside" and "outside" should include psychic as well as organic structure. And since psychic structure comprises internalizations built up over the course of one's personal history, including their affective tone, it would be reasonable to include affective resonances from the past as well as the current reality.

Affective resonances must begin in the intimacy of the infant–caretaker ambience. Endowed with a biologically based expressive quality of perception, the infant is pre-tuned to respond to sentient shapes of *tension* and *release*; that is to say, patterns of tension and release occurring in sequences of *timing*. The interplay between infant and care-taker is characterized by corresponding patterns of timed sequences of tension and release—a formal congruence that signals their mutuality. Tension and release being at the heart of affect, we may postulate that it is the subjective experience of such congruence that gives rise to affective resonances. (More later.)

We may now attempt a more comprehensive statement about *congruence* and the *qualities* of experience: in an interactive open system between our psychobiological selves and our encounter with the world—including those aspects of the past that remain dynamically active—the experience of congruence between temporal patterns of tension and release in self and world gives rise to responsive affective resonances that infuse or shape the quality of experience.

That there is a circularity in this account is undeniable: the experience of the world is based on the view of our experience. Philosophically, this reflects a post-Kantian world wherein the structures of reality are subordinate to those of the knowing subject; in that the observer helps create and curtail the world of perception, there is an unbridge-able gap between the human realm and actual existence.

Psychologically, this circularity reflects early development. In the course of repetitive responsive interplay of timed patterns of tension and release between infant and caretaker, this interactive field is internalized, projected, and reinternalized. As a result, internal and external worlds are cast *in part* in terms of each other as corresponding intrapsychic internalizations of affective–sentient patterns of tension and release.

Though circular, postulating emotional resonances between congruent structures in self and world accords equal status to inside and outside. It avoids the (modernist and postmodernist) excesses of an omnipotent subjectivism that depreciates the value of the external world; or, the opposite, a despairing materialism alienated from human qualities (Sass, 1992).

It also encourages one to search for congruent structures on either side of the essentially unbridgeable gap between inside and outside. Turning back once again to music as our port of entry, we therefore ask: of the innumerable intrapsychic representations of self and world that exist in anyone's mind, which ones might have the formal attributes that would make them likely to "resonate" with the nature of music?

Everything we have learned about music being rooted both outside and inside, transcending the linguistic and other boundaries between subjectivity and objectivity, necessarily makes us look in the direction of intrapsychic representations that have the character of *merged boundaries* between internal and external. Obviously, from the point of view of development, this must refer to some of the earliest stages of learning to differentiate self from (m)other.

Now it is true that direct observation of behavioral interaction between mothers and very young infants has shown a wide range of relational capacities that indicate the infant has some degree of cognitive awareness of *separateness* from the mother. However, in contrast to actual behavioral interaction, *intrapsychic* representations, on the other hand, comprise various degrees and kinds of persisting *undifferentiation* of infant from mother. These coexist with representations of clear and increasing differentiation.

Two primary types of intrapsychic *un*differentiation, or symbiotic relatedness between infant-mother, have been described (Blatt and Shichman, 1983; Blatt and Blass, 1990; Blass and Blatt, unpublished paper). The following summarizes some salient features.

The distinction between the two types of symbiotic relatedness between infant and mother depends on whether attachment or separateness tends to predominate. In the attachment mode the self representation is more or less *lost* in its *union* with the maternal representation. In the separateness mode the self representation expands to *include* the maternal representation.

In the course of time, while remaining relatively undifferentiated, normally these two modes continue to develop, interact in an ongoing dialectic with each other, and contribute to two distinctive styles of relating to others throughout a lifetime. The attachment–union style contributes to stable interpersonal relatedness, with the tendency to seek harmony and synthesis. It focuses more on affects and visual images, and prefers simultaneous modes of thought. (Pathologically it tends to correlate with anaclitic depression and hysterical syndromes.)

The separateness mode of intrapsychic symbiotic relatedness contributes to autonomy and a consolidated definition of self. It tends toward sequential modes of thinking. (Pathologically, it is inclined toward introjective depression, paranoid, obsessive–compulsive, and phallic narcissistic syndromes.)

Both modes of intrapsychic symbiotic relatedness should coexist and be integrated with well-delineated self and object representations in order to avoid detriment to an individual's realistic perception of self and others. Most relevant to our purpose, it is this overall integration within one's self-identity that makes possible the capacity for intense emotional experience—in love, religion, and the arts.

Returning now to music in the light of the foregoing. In that music exists in an intermediate area between inside and outside, are there sentient forms in music that lend themselves to the illusion of being emotionally *attuned* to intrapsychic modes of symbiotic relatedness? Conversely, how might a composer—preconsciously or unconsciously—draw upon his own developmental lines of separateness and attachment within a symbiotic matrix to find congruent musical forms?

Recall the two morphologies of symbiotic relatedness in a developmental dialectic with each other: the attachment-union form (self merged within other in a union of *sameness*); the separateness form (self expanded to include other, preserving a degree of *difference*). The formal structural attribute—sameness—is thus embodied within the psychological idea of attachment-union. Likewise, the formal element, difference, is embodied within the psychological notion of separateness. We may now seek examples in music of an interplay between *sameness* and *difference*, corresponding in this inner form to the psychological dialectic between the two different internalizations of symbiotic relatedness: *attachment-union* and *separateness*, associated in turn with release and tension, respectively.

Musical syntax and composition offer many examples of sameness-difference or unity-separateness in benevolent coexistence—corresponding, one might say, on a psychological plane, with symbiotic types of relatedness of the attachment-union and separateness varieties.

Without implying a compendium, the following may at least be mentioned. In octaves and scales, the same relationship of tones to each other coexists with difference in registers. In the various tonalities, the relationship of tones to each other remains the same in different keys. In musical spelling, the same note may be "spelled" in different ways; for example, E-flat or D-sharp, to indicate different potential relationships to other keys. (An example of tonal ambiguity possibly standing for psychological conflict: cf. S. Feder [1993a], on Schubert's *Moment Musical*, Opus 94, #6[D780].) In chords, the distinctness of each separate tone is preserved within the unity of the whole.

Regarding various types of musical composition, both the sonata and the concerto may be taken as musical examples of the interplay of sameness and difference, corresponding to the attachment–union and separateness modes of internalization of symbiotic relatedness between mother and child. In the exposition portion of the solo sonato, the second theme moves to the dominant (if in the major mode), or to the relative major (if in the minor mode). This degree of destabilization provides contrast, polarity, and tension. But then, in the recapitulation section, all themes have modulated back to the tonic home base, providing unification, stability, and resolution in a "marriage" that has united differences while preserving contrasts.

The concerto form offers another example of the interplay of separateness and unity. Thanks largely to Mozart, the concerto idea became a showpiece for two different kinds of contrast between a solo instrument and the orchestra (*tutti*): either one of contention (root: concertáre) or of collaboration (root: conserère). Mozart wrote only two piano concertos in minor keys, the D-Minor (K. 466) and the C-Minor (K. 491), in both of which contention predominates over collaboration.

Before going into a musical discussion of these it will be useful to place them in the context of Mozart's well-known contention–collaboration, attachment–separation relationship with his father—one that deserves to stand as a prime example of a dialectic between the two types of symbiotic relatedness we have outlined.

Mozart married Constanze Weber in Vienna on August 4, 1782, prior to the arrival of his father Leopold's long withheld and still unwilling consent. Almost immediately after the birth of their first child in June 1783, the couple journeyed to Salzburg to present Constanze to Leopold. During their three-month stay, neither father Leopold, nor sister Nannerl, ever became reconciled to the match.

During the late summer of 1784 Mozart had a serious illness consistent with rheumatic fever or a poststreptococcal kidney disease, glomerulonephritis (Davies, 1993). Before the year was out another child, Karl, was born and that winter, February 11, 1785, father came for a two-month visit to Vienna.

Mozart wrote the K. 466 piano concerto in anticipation of this visit, completing it the day before his father's arrival. It was one of the few compositions he did in D-Minor (a key "biographically related to father, fathering, and fatherhood and affects of rage and vengeance" [S. Feder, 1993b, p. 129]).

The meeting proved to be their last, for Leopold's health began to fail soon after his return to Salzburg. He died *two years* later (May 28, 1787). Mozart completed the second of his two minor key piano concertos, K. 491, in C-Minor, two years after his own serious illness and a year before father died.

Of the two years between Leopold's visit and his death (comprising the two minor key piano concertos), Mozart wrote to his father on his deathbed: "As death is . . . the true end and aim of our lives, I have for the last *two years* made myself so well acquainted with this true, best friend of man-

kind that his image no longer terrifies, but calms and con-
soles me. . . . I never lie down to rest without thinking that,
young as I am, before the dawn of another day I may be no
more" (Blom, 1954, p. 944; emphasis added). He did, in
fact, die within five years.

Mozart's commending death as mankind's "best friend,"
when his father lay dying, parallels and contrasts ironically
with an earlier letter of Leopold extolling a father as a
child's best friend: "There is no true friend—. . . *in its fullest sense*–but a father. Even children are not *in the same
degree* friends towards their own parents" (Anderson, 1938,
p. 598).

Turning now to a discussion of the two minor key piano
concertos (for which I am wholly indebted to Deirdre
O'Donohue and her unpublished paper), the solo's *conflict*
with the *tutti* is intensified by a unique feature: in the first
movement of each, the solo's first themes, intimate and poignant, are never taken up by the orchestra. Nor are they
ever alluded to in the respective recapitulations by the
orchestra. They are, indeed, formally "lost." But their
real, external absence may only serve to dramatize their ef-
fective, internal, psychic presence, consciously or preconsciously, in performers and audience alike.

Further heightening this weighty "presence of an absence" of the solo's first themes in both concertos is the
fact that the secondary thematic material, in dramatic contrast, is handled *collaboratively* by orchestra and soloist.

In the first movements of these concertos Mozart deals
differently with the dialectic of separateness and togeth-
erness of solo and *tutti*: while the solo's first *themes* are
never again alluded to in either K. 466 or K. 491, the solo
voice, at least, does return in the coda of K. 491, rejoining
the *tutti* in collaboration with it. This is a singular departure from classic form where usually, following the solo's

display in the cadenza, the orchestra has the stage to it-self.

Numerous examples in music may be adduced as to the ongoing dialectic there between sameness and difference, attachment-unity and separateness. Loss and presence deserves special mention. For dealing with loss would seem to be inherent in the nature of music. Not only in the special case of the "lost" first themes of Mozart's two minor key piano concertos, but in the more prosaic matter of musical rests. By their very nature, rests seem to hang suspended at the edge of memory. Imposing external silence, they impel psychic inwardness. Is it too much to suggest that this is redolent with latent memory "in the deep heart's core?" Overriding the distinction between presence and loss, inside and outside, the "music" of absent voices within resonates to the silence—restoring a measure of the fullness of early time.

When Gauguin draws upon persisting personal ambiguities—gender identity sameness and difference—he paints androgynous forms embedded in vibrating "musical" harmonies of color.

When Mozart draws upon his own psychological identity themes—separateness and attachment, union and loss—he transforms them into musical shapes of solo and *tutti* in mutual contention and collaboration. Or he totally drops a poignant theme without any working through, despatching it to a premature silence that affirms, while the memory of it denies, the premonition of his own mortality; conjoined, perhaps, as in life, with father's?

Thus the arts transform lifetime existential and personal developmental challenges into abstract universal forms in a dynamic balance of tension and release. Tension and release also constitute the central dynamic of emotion, the congruence between aesthetic forms and emotion becomes the basis for emotional resonance. Feelings, then, resonate to aesthetic forms which, by giving them external shape, *seem* to be attuned to "witness" and enhance realities inside and out.

And between.

The question arises: is there a neurophysiological correlate at best, or metaphor at least, that may help us to think about the "in-between-ness" of affective awareness?

THE NEW YORK TIMES (March 21, 1995, pp. C-1 and C-10) reports a discovery that may be relevant: relay stations in the thalamus, a central brain structure, send out waves of nervous impulses that scan the streams of sensory data coming in from each sense. Since these data are distributed all across the cortex, how do they become bound together into single images? The theory is that they are *entrained temporally*; that is, they are brought into the same swing or synchrony with the rhythm of the thalamic scanning waves.

Some neuroscientists hold that this temporal synchrony or binding may explain the nature of consciousness. Since the thalamus plays a key role in coordinating the impulses that constitute affect, might not this model of temporal scanning and entrainment to a single rhythm serve for affective awareness: an interplay of resonance and attunement?

5

THE INTERPLAY OF RESONANCE
AND ATTUNEMENT

Not long before he died, the painter Robert Motherwell (1991) said: "the game is not what things look like. The game is organizing states of feeling, [which] become questions of light, color, solidity, airiness, lyricism, whatever."

Almost one hundred years earlier, Paul Gauguin (quoted by Tardieu, 1895) had written: "[I] arrang[e] lines and colors . . . that represent nothing absolutely real . . . ; but they compel us to reflect . . . simply by means of the mysterious affinities that exist between our brain and those arrangements of colors and lines." He believed that "a given arrangement of colors, lights, and shadows"—"the music of the painting"—constituted a "magical harmony" that "seized" one in a "dreamy" emotional way before one ever gets to the "down-to-earth" details of whatever it is the painting is "about."

Plainly, there are relationships between arrangements of colors, lines, tones in art, and the emotions that resonate in response. But we lack the key of a language between brain and mind to answer, in suitable form, How do external perceptual stimuli in the artwork impinge on

79

the brain and become transmuted into internal affective states in the mind/body?

What can psychoanalysis *say*, not *tell*, to help clarify these "mysterious affinities"; emotional resonances in mutual interplay with the attunement of aesthetic forms?

Let us make two assumptions: (1) the aesthetic alliance is analogous to the therapeutic alliance; (2) the structure of art and the emotions are homologous.

Analogy

The ambience of the aesthetic alliance and the therapeutic alliance both facilitate emotional responsiveness. Not unlike the early holding environment, they are attuned to emotional responsiveness in a double respect: (1) the freedom for one to experience a full range of feelings; but (2) within the security of a stable structure.

A few general remarks will suffice at this point.

The structure of art offers familiarity, knowledge, and security together with imaginative freedom and ambiguity. The combination invites feelingful responses in the course of imaginative wanderings while guaranteeing a safe return. Knowledge and imagination, each in the service of the other, blend realistic constraints with an invitation to conscious and unconscious feelings and memories rooted in psychological issues of one's own personal history.

The therapeutic situation, too, is conducive to a readiness for conscious and unconscious feeling-memory and the formation of transferences. It aims at being attuned to shifting balances of closeness and distance, while providing the assurance that neither gratification nor punishment but compassionate neutrality will greet the verbal expression of all thoughts and feelings (Rose, 1992, pp. 219–220).

Homology

The idea of homologous structures usually referred to as isomorphism, was first proposed by Arnheim (1949) as part of a Gestalt study of expression. For example, a visual stimulus results in a configuration of electrochemical forces in the corticolimbic circuitry; this in turn determines psychological experience as counterparts such as mood or movement. Various types of experience—visual, kinesthetic or emotional—seem to elicit similar electrocortical patterns, suggesting that one global percept may be coded in different sensory modules according to isomorphic patterns. The idea of isomorphism has been carried over into the field of linguistics (Jakobson and Waugh, 1979); dance has been described as an external spatialization of the temporal structure of music (Kapferer, 1983); S. Feder (1990) analyzed a song of Charles Ives, musically as well as psychobiographically, to show that its internal musical structure "mirrors the mental organization underlying the affect [of nostalgia]" (p. 265).

The statement of homology or isomorphism most useful for the present discussion has to do with the relationship between the emotionally expressive composition of art and the emotional responsiveness of a recipient. More specifically, tension and release, built into the work of art, corresponds to a sensitivity to tension and release which is a primary attribute of perception—its expressive quality. The expressive quality of feelingful perception does not focus on "the static aspects of shape, size, hue, or pitch, which can be measured with some yardstick, but on the *directed tensions* conveyed by these same stimuli" (Arnheim, 1966, p. 313; emphasis added).

Apprehending the earth in terms of its perceived qualities of tension and release, one evaluates it for what it provides in the way of "affordances" (Gibson, 1979) for good or ill. Such global perception of the qualitative aspects of stimuli involves a process of matching, comparing, remembering with feeling, and an inherent bodily awareness, namely affect.

At first Freud related affect with life energy. Until "The Ego and the Id" (1923), "energy" was instinctual energy, and feelings were vicissitudes of libidinal energy. Later he came to understand unpleasure as due to conflict, and speculated that pleasure depended on qualitative rises and falls of excitation such as rhythm (1924). With "Inhibitions, Symptoms and Anxiety" (1926), signal anxiety was a response by the ego to danger arising *either* from instinct or the real world.

Brierley (1937) developed the idea that affects are essentially tension phenomena pressing for discharge, rather than discharge itself. Jacobson (1971), prefiguring later developments, described feelings as rises and falls of tension around a central axis, the quality "depending on . . . the amount of excitation and the speed and rhythm of discharge" (p. 28).

The important points for our present purpose are: (1) We are dealing with the idea that *patterns* of *tension* and *resolution* underlie the hedonic sensations that constitute the inner dynamic of emotion. (2) Patterns of tension and release likewise constitute the inner structure of aesthetic form. More precisely, the actual organic sensations of tension-release in a person having an emotional response to art correspond with (i.e., match in structural organization) the equilibria of virtual tensions and release in the inorganic art sample.

Visual art and music are largely a matter of directions and forces. This is more readily apparent in music than visual art since music is wholly nonmaterial and involved with *purely* dynamic phenomena. Hearing music is above all hearing ordered motion, and "right or wrong in music is not a matter of pitch as such but of pitch in relation to the direction of motion" (Zuckerkandl, 1956, p. 81).

Just as a visual artist knows how to enhance the expressive qualities inherent in ordinary visual perception, a musical composer does likewise with auditory perception (e.g., simple repetition, modulating from one key to another, delaying a closure, ornamentation, and so on). The art literature is full of allusions to this core dynamic of tension and release. As Dewey (1934, p. 207) noted long ago, any artist selects, intensifies, and composes the quality of experience in such a way as to express it more energetically and clearly than the original from which it was extracted (cf. Rose, 1992, pp. 207–212).

Exploring Emotional Resonances

When an artist builds virtual tension and release into an aesthetic structure, he or she is not necessarily communicating his or her own feelings. Nor is a viewer, responding with actual tension and release, necessarily "reading" the artist's own emotions. Let us say, rather, that art invites an interplay based on the congruence of homologous structures noted earlier: between the virtual tension and release patterns in the art object and one's own actual patterns of tension and release responding to the art object. As this interplay between tension patterns becomes intensified, it tends to activate itself and become amplified (Tomkins, 1980). The concurrent emotion is what is referred to here as "emotional resonances," which draw on: (1) embedded reactions to shapes of stimulation; (2) affective signaling; and (3) the interplay of imagination and knowledge.

Embedded Reactions to Shapes of Stimulation

Many years of experimental work by Silvan Tomkins (1962–1963, 1980, 1981) carry forward earlier workers' intuitions that *degrees* of tension not only lay at the heart of affect but that the *profile* of the stimulation determines *which* affect. Whatever is new, constant, or ceases, commands attention and elicits different emotional responses. Tomkins distinguished nine innate effects according to whether stimulation increases, stays constant, or decreases.

To summarize some of his work: from the first day of life, an optimal degree of sound, light, or touch stimulation will elicit facial interest from the baby. More than optimal stimulation causes surprise at first, and then distress, anger, and fear. A sharp rise in stimulation followed by a sudden drop will bring an expression of joy.

From the earliest days of life it appears that infants not only react to the contour of stimulation but also translate information received in one sensory modality into another and respond with analogous affects. Significantly, the ultimate reference for the match is not the external event but the inner feeling state (Stern, 1985, p. 138).

Do such embedded and transmodal "emotional resonances" require symbolic transformations or can they be induced directly? There are mixed views on this question.

An analytic view is that peak-affect states occurring in connection with very pleasurable or painful experiences, organize memory structures that "may spur the earliest symbolic activities, in that one element . . . stands for the entire constellation [of light, sound, and rhythm]. . . . A light turned on in a room, for example, [may signify] the presence of the feeding mother even before she herself is perceived" (Kernberg, 1992, p. 16).

On the other hand, work with adult experimental sub-

jects (Clynes and Nettheim, 1982) indicates that characteristic dynamic expressive forms in various sensory modes can
induce specific emotions directly. For example, there are
distinct finger pressure patterns that correspond to various
emotions (anger, hate, grief, love, sex, joy, reverence). On
seeing a videotape of a hand and part of the forearm pro-
ducing these dynamic pressure patterns, experimental subjects correctly recognized the emotions these pressure
patterns represent. Their record of correct choices corre-
sponded to a one in ten million expectancy by chance alone.

When these videotapes were then fed into an analog com-
puter to convert the touch (motoric) expressive forms into
sound forms (amplitude and frequency) of the same emotionally expressive quality, subjects, including forty Central
Australian aborigines, again correctly identified the emotion represented by the sound patterns to a similarly high
degree of statistical significance.

Affective Signaling

These findings lend themselves to integration with our own
discussion. The preverbal infant makes use of inborn affective reactions and transmodal emotional resonances in the
course of daily handling and intuitive play. What we have
earlier referred to as the expressive quality of perception—
the capacity to perceive with feeling—refers to embedded
emotional resonances to dynamic sentient patterns of stimulation.

The sentient shapes of pressure and sound identified as
corresponding to various emotions correlate with the affective signals that pass between the infant and its earliest
caretakers. Such affective signaling may be thought of as
another kind of (interpersonal) emotional resonance. It

constitutes the communicational matrix between infant and caretaker. Like the structure of aesthetic form, it is also organized around an optimal degree of tension and resolution. Nor can it be a coincidence that, from birth on, the *musical* aspects of speech are the ones that most compel the infant's attention: rhythm and timing at first, then, by 6 months, the variations of intonation and a tonal range at a particular pitch (Panel, 1980). Nor can it be coincidence that parents across cultures automatically exaggerate the *musical* features of speech in sing-songing to the infant (Emde, 1983, pp. 171–172). The baby, responding in kind well before 6 months of age, can match the pitch, intensity, melodic contour, and rhythmic structure of mother's songs.

This biologically based *open* system of affective signaling between parent and infant is like a dance. It is comprised largely of tonal (and visual) repetitiveness (establishment and aversion of gaze), and soothing familiarity perked with graded doses of excitement. It is fine-tuned to the shifting nuances in the baby's needs for closeness or distance, separateness or reunion—all geared toward providing stimulation while avoiding traumatic intensities of affect. Such emotional availability, expressed through rhythmicity of interchange and matching, leads to an attachment between infant and caretaker, and is the central growth promoting factor on which the baby's well-being depends (Stern, 1985).

When sensitivity to such qualities as stimulus intensity, contour, rhythm, and duration are evoked much later in life in the experience of art, it becomes understandable why:

> [T]hese shapes or semblances . . . seem ineffable. . . . [while M]any of the components of the network, especially the motor/ emotional ones, may not be accessible to . . . linguistic interpretation and . . . consciousness. . . . They [nevertheless] can produce emotional responses that are compelling, insidious, and

expressive because they elude the usual interpretive verbal explanations and instead set up *resonances* among other . . . nonverbal sensory/emotional representations [Dissanayake, 1992, p. 157; emphasis added].

Imagination and Knowledge

Affective signaling and embedded reactions to shapes of stimuli provide the *preverbal* backdrop for the child's "primary affectivity." While this recedes with time (language, defense mechanisms, and self-awareness), aspects remain unconsciously to influence one's general emotional responsiveness (Wilson and Malatesta, 1989).

But each person's emotional responsiveness is likely to be unique rather than conforming to a population norm. This is because of the constant interplay of (primary process) imagination with (secondary process) knowledge of reality, as well as the triggering of associated ideas and memories.

Each of us processes all data in two fundamentally different ways simultaneously: imaginatively and realistically. They follow different rules of organization. (Primary process) imagination deals with data along holistic lines, with wide angle, low focus, broad strokes, using condensation, displacement, and symbolism. (Secondary process) knowledge of reality has to do with delineated, narrow angle, high focused, realistic modes of organization.

Holistic, imaginative modes of organization are associated with a release of tension; delineated, realistic modes of organization are associated with a buildup of tension. Hence, the interplay of playful, imaginative freedom with the constraints of realistic boundaries generates a flow of tension and release that is conducive to emotional resonances.

Art, moreover, demands and stimulates more than ordinary perception. Insofar as it consists of a dynamically balanced concentration of virtual rhythms culled from ordinary perception and experience, it stimulates an *enhanced* interplay of imagination and knowledge. With this goes heightened currents of tension and release. Thus, a much greater propensity for emotional resonances as wholes dissolve into parts; new integrations are reconstituted again and again; the strange is discovered in the midst of the familiar; the old within the new.

Symbolism and metaphor, rhetoric and the arts, tap the *freedom* of primary process imaginative forms of organization and exploit it within the problem-solving *constraints* of secondary process knowledge of reality. The interplay of imaginative freedom and realistic constraints potentiates an emotional response in accordance with the particular issues associatively triggered in each of us.

Among the general issues are mourning and memorializing, as well as the reconciliation of familiarity with strangeness, temporal continuity and change, spatial synthesis and separateness. By so doing, art symbolically fulfills opposite urges: to individuate and separate (associated with rising tension), and to draw back toward some form of irredentist reunion (associated with falling tension). Being part of the human condition, and probably inherent in the growth process, these issues are never "resolved." Potentially available to respond to any current stimulus, these universal themes reverberate especially to the forms of art (Rose, 1980, 1987).

Theoretically there is hardly any limit to the depth of feeling-memories that are "on tap" to lend a richness of personal emotional response to the *nonverbal* ambience of aesthetically balanced tension and release. In the beginning, thinking and feeling are facets of a total experience. Memories are stored in association with the dominant feelings of the moment and may gain consciousness when the original feelings are rearoused

The structural basis for this is that affects, sensations, and memory functions are processed by the same or parallel neuroanatomical corticolimbic circuits and structures with interconnecting shunts (Reiser, 1990). Each may stimulate the others. Usually this occurs without awareness or we would be flooded. Sensations stir old feelings and lost memories (see Chapter 2).

Freud's Reaction to Michelangelo's "Moses"

According to our formulation, a constant interplay of imagination and realistic cognition generates a flow of tension and release conducive to emotional resonances. Since art concentrates the dynamics of ordinary perception, it is possible that the *enhanced* interplay of imagination and knowledge associated with art may account for the emotional responsiveness to art, with or without the unconscious recruitment of earlier sources of emotional resonance, namely, embedded reactions to shapes of stimuli and affective signaling between parent and caretaker.

There is also another possibility: a *hypertrophy* of the disciplined *cognitive* component as it interplays with imagination may result in conflicting impulses that inhibit emotional resonances.

Something of this sort is suggested by Freud's reactions to Michelangelo's "Moses." As is well known, he hesitated for years before publishing his paper on this statue; then did so anonymously; and waited eleven more years before putting his name to it. In addition, he channeled his powerful response to the "Moses" ("No piece of statuary has ever made a stronger impression on me" [Freud, 1914, p. 213]), *away* from his own personal emotional reactions and onto Michelangelo's motivation in sculpting it.

"Whenever I cannot [explain the effect of art], as for instance with music, I am almost incapable of obtaining any pleasure," wrote Freud (1914, p. 211).

> Some rationalistic . . . turn of mind in me rebels against being moved by a thing without knowing why I am thus affected. . . . In my opinion, what grips us so powerfully can only be the artist's *intention* . . . to awaken in us the same emotional attitude . . . as that which in him produced the impetus to create. . . . To discover his intention, though, I must first find out the meaning and . . . be able to *interpret it* [pp. 211–212].

In "The Moses of Michelangelo" Freud imagined that Michelangelo was imagining a particular point in history when Moses saw the Israelites dancing around the Golden Calf and was enraged. In contrast to many writers, beginning in the seventeenth century, who saw Moses as being about to rise and denounce his followers (Liebert, 1983), and to scripture itself which speaks of his smashing the tablets of the law, Freud "saw" Moses as controlling his wrath and preserving them. Evidently it resonated so closely with his own rage—screening early losses and ambivalences—that he responded defensively. He buffered his aesthetic response by speculating about Michelangelo's intention and interposing this narrative between the impact of the statue and his own response.

It is likely that Freud's narrative recreation "completed" Michelangelo's "Moses" in a way consonant with his own dynamics and current stresses (Fuller, 1980). Freud first encountered the "Moses" at a time when he was being angrily rejected by his then father substitute, Wilhelm Fliess.

At the time of writing the paper a dozen years later he was beset with similar problems of backsliding followers, Adler and Jung, and his own father-figure loyalties, Brücke and Helmholtz, from whose logical positivism he was moving away in his own writing ("On Narcissism" [1914]).

A recent paper suggests that, had Freud explored his own strong affects, he might have been drawn into a personal realm of intense early preoedipal losses and yearnings between the ages of 1 and 3 (Goldsmith, 1992). (It is also likely that these issues lay at the root of his inability to enjoy music.) Instead, he (defensively) explored oedipal concerns with fathers and sons. Recent research also indicates that his fundamental ambivalence regarding his Jewish identity and early grounding in Judaism may well have played a role in his reactions (Rice, 1990; Spitz, 1989; Yerushalmi, 1991).

Whatever the private facts may have been concerning either Freud or Michelangelo, the statue is a monumental portrayal of controlled tension between potential action and restraint. This alone creates ambiguity—witness the contrast between the traditional view that Moses was about to express his rage and Freud's seeing Moses (and himself) as controlling his rage. There is no way to judge between these alternatives or any other subjective responses; each is valid in its own right.

The relevant aesthetic issue is not one of accurately deducing Michelangelo's *intention* but his success in presenting any viewer with the necessary sensory wherewithal to have his or her own particular emotional response. The artistically created balance of mighty bodily tensions stimulates in the viewer an empathic bodily identification with corresponding tensions. On a different level, a resonating interplay of imagination and knowledge provides another source of feelings or—as illustrated by Freud's reaction to Michelangelo's "Moses"—a partial defense against them.

The "Attunement" of Art

As this example illustrates, art is ultimately "realized," if at all, in receptive minds, and even then only along the lines permitted by the receiver's defensive filters. These obviously place limits on the power of art to engender, as Diderot and Kant noted, much that is not contained within itself, even urging the mind beyond experience. The interplay of knowledge and imagination stimulated by art—with the associated flow of tension and release experienced as affect—is limited by the mind of the receiver.

And there is the spirit of the times. It is a truism that each era sees and hears in its own way. Much that pleases us would have been considered harsh and dissonant to a nineteenth century audience. Some of this is due to the fact that many of their established musical meanings no longer speak to us because we are ignorant of the relevant conventions (Neubauer, 1986, p. 58). In addition, sensibilities do change; the past undergoes revision; special interest groups politicize taste.

Bach's music "is" far more now than during his lifetime. His son, C. P. E. Bach, considered monumental in his own time, "is" much less now. In the thirties, Clifford Odets was being called the American Chekhov only to have become "irrelevant," and he is just now being revived. Odet's personal sense of disinheritance cogwheeled with the collective sense of disinheritance in the Depression era, making him the personal spokesman for many in his audience of that time; now, this has begun to happen again (Brenman-Gibson, 1981).

Postponing for now consideration of whether or how an *individual* may make "use" of art—apart from or within the prevailing *zeitgeist*—the potential of art to seem to attune itself resiliently to one's changing needs endows it with the quality of seeming to be responsively "alive."

This is in sharp contrast with the one-dimensionality or out-of-tuneness of other experiences. Schreber's sadomaso-chistic psychosis is a useful example of out-of-tuneness. Both pornography and social activist art, as compared to erotic art and art in general, are instances of one-dimensionality.

In *Memoirs of My Nervous Illness*, Daniel Paul Schreber (1903) presented a remarkable account of his tormented relationship to God. It boils down to the sadomasochistic interdependence between his "nerves" and God's "rays." "Nerves," he explained, are the foundation of human ex-perience, their "vibrations" corresponding to conscious-ness. (Note the resemblance, pp. 60–61, to Freud's idea in the "Project" that consciousness is the awareness of the subjective qualities resulting from neuronal motion cor-responding to rhythm, tone, or oscillation of the neural wave impinging on the sense organs.) "Nerves" vibrate to external impressions and to the "rays" emanating from God—rays being the nerves of God. Too much attraction between God and Schreber can threaten the former with annihilation; too little attraction threatens the latter with abandonment.

It has been argued recently (Sass, 1992) that God's rays may be interpreted as representing a (partially internalized) observing other, and that Schreber's nerves represent the self as an object of observation. Further, that this splitting of the self into an observing subject and object observed "might perhaps stand as a metaphor for modern subjectiv-ity in general" (p. 260), as exemplified in Paul Valéry's fic-tional character, Monsieur Teste.

Bringing this in line with our present discussion, Schre-ber's nerves might stand for one psychotic person's exces-sive responsiveness to the rays, standing for the dynamic shapes of sentient hyperstimulation originally emanating from the external world. While such an unmodulated *dis-*

equilibrium between self and world would essentially stem from an intrapsychic failure of ego regulation, it might also be viewed as a metaphor of affective signaling gone awry. In either case, the result is an experience of lurching out of control in opposite directions—the threat of a Self obliterating an Other alternating with that of being totally abandoned by the Other.

The "intercourse" between Schreber's nerves and God's rays was clearly sadomasochistic. The unmodulated aggression is inherent in the double threat of annihilation and abandonment. Moreover, Schreber would complain bitterly and explicitly of often experiencing great "voluptuousness." Therefore, Schreber's psychosis may well be contrasted to its sadomasochistic analogue in art, namely, pornography. The sexual and aggressive "rush" in both pornography and Schreber's psychosis are manifestations of disregulation, unbalancing or defusion of sexual and aggressive impulses. They both thus stand in contrast to erotic art.

The defusion of the sexual and the aggressive in pornography is manifested in the splitting off of the tender from the erotic. Since sexual and aggressive components of emotional life are polarized rather than integrated, human organisms are in effect reduced to bodily organs. Finally, the habitual use of pornography often represents the annihilation of the humanity of the other as a vengeful and hungry reaction to past dehumanization and emotional impoverishment—both likely possibilities for Schreber from what we now know of his early experience at the hands of his father (Niederland, 1959).

In contrast to pornography, the content of erotic art shows a higher level of emotional maturity in psychosexual development and object relations. Erotic art orchestrates early sexual components into an enriched, complex, nuanced experience of sexual union in the context of object love, idealization, and a mutual tolerance of differences (Kernberg, 1993).

However, the maturity standard alone fails to tell us what makes erotic art *art* and not just a celebration of erotic subject matter within the fulsomeness of maturity. Older views notwithstanding, it cannot be sheer beauty either that makes erotic art succeed in transcending everyday reality, as witness the well-established place of ugliness in art from Hieronymous Bosch to the modern era. As love transcends needful attachment, or wisdom mere intelligence, art exceeds beauty even with the psychological additives of psychosexual maturity plus the capacity for true object relationships.

Comparing erotic art—as art—to pornography and Schreber's sadomasochistic psychosis we find a marriage that works. Whether the content is primarily representational or abstract, sexual or nonsexual, art creates a new wholeness out of different constituents. Yet, while form and content are inseparable, contrasting elements are preserved. It may be this reconciliation of integrity with diversity that places an artwork in apparent attunement with one's own sense of wholeness *and* shifting states—simultaneously. It neither oscillates rigidly between polar extremes (Schreber), nor proffers a one-way rapid express regression (pornography).

It should be mentioned parenthetically in this connection that the prioritizing of the id, in the case of pornography, is not unlike the effect of the opposite tilt in the direction of the superego in the case of social activist art. Using art *primarily* as the excuse for a blow-out of either instinctual impulses or moral propaganda—and it was Freud who pointed out the secret alliances that can form between id and superego—leads to similar effects: boredom and exhaustion of the senses.

The superegoism of political activist art leads to no stylistic innovation or intellectual stimulation but only facile communication and simplistic stereotyping (Kuspit, 1993). The crushing tyranny of its moral imperative was well captured during the Khruschev era when, in response to a question from a visiting western artist, an art commissar defined social realism as "socialism plus the reality of Soviet Power."

In contrast to such monolithic boredom and depletion, erotic art, like art in general, *refreshes* the senses. It opens up the realm of imaginative *forms* in a play of mutual interpenetration with content. Form and content may embody or balance each other, as well as carry meaning on different levels.

Often what is iconographically encoded or surreptitiously alluded to in Western art is frankly exposed in fine Eastern erotica of India, China, and Japan. On the other hand, in Eastern erotic art the tranquil facial expressions of the lovemaking couple while coupling may well give pause to a viewer's erotic responsivity. Attention is diverted to the tastefully furnished room or landscape, with birds and plants. There may be food set out, and cooking and cosmetic implements. Nor is the viewer alone. Musicians, attendants, aides may (also) be present and in a similar state of apparent detachment. The viewer is invited to join and become part of the overall aesthetic integration of the scene—the subject matter of which happens to be erotic.

The emphasis on composition, balance, and harmony reflects the philosophy of the underlying culture. For example, the Kama Sutra of India, composed between the second and fifth centuries, A.D., is one of the earliest attempts to define the relationship between man and woman. Since the sexual act is at the heart of this relationship, the Kama Sutra sets out to answer the question of with whom, under what circumstances, and how. It being the

An acrobatic variation of a love position from the *Kama Sutra*.

duty of a married man to make love to his wife, and since there is merit to be gained from doing so, there is more merit to be gained from doing it well. *But,* the aim of sensuous, including sexual, pleasure (Kama) must be pursued in harmony with the other great aims of life: moral duty (Dharma), and amassing possessions (Artha) for the benefit of one's family, including learning and skills, without which it would be just opportunism and materialism.

The aesthetic integration of erotic art is seen in the fact that all the *forms*–erotic and nonerotic alike–may come to be seen in time as mirroring and rhyming with one another in a pleasurable suspension of dynamically balanced tension and release without discharge. Lavish ornamentation, humor, comic relief, social context and commentary, the serene expressions of the lovers–all may be used to diffract the attention further and invite leisurely reflection overall. The highly charged, even blatant, sexuality–filtered through forms and overall compositions–succeeds in suffusing the entire scene with contained energy. And remains sexual, too.

The whole picture that unfolds is there to be experienced in many ways, including but not limited to pure abstraction of interweaving Matisselike forms and/or frank sex. Moreover, each way of experiencing may oscillate with the others. The initial sensual–sexual turn-on to the erotic *content* may blend into an involvement with all the forms *as forms*– qualitatively transformed into the realm of the sensuous-aesthetic experience. The visual experience may become abstract.

How has this come about? The underlying affectomotor core of experience–with all its sexual and aggressive driven quality–has been drawn upon and blended with forms that have been idealized, relatively desexualized, transposed, and resexualized, and thereby delayed and diffused.

Perception, however, has not been neutered into blandness. On the contrary, it has become energized with a quality of fresh feeling and wide range. The primitive sensuous affectomotor strivings that exist in the nonverbal reaches of psychic life—"normally" left unattended in the course of every-dailiness—have been reintegrated on another level. Liberating, exploring, elaborating, and reintegrating them may well be the central concern of all art, a measure of its success, a source of its power to revivify as well as transcend.

Matisse's art, for example, though not generally thought of as primarily erotic, seems to derive to some extent from his highly libidinized relationship to his mother. A persuasive argument has been made that he used idealization and abstraction to regulate his sense of being instinctively overstimulated by woman's flesh (Kuspit, 1993).

Having discovered the "revelation" of the Orient and Islamic art, he rediscovered for himself the shape of the arabesque. It is an ornament composed essentially of abstract elements:

> The field is geometrically parcelled out in . . . circles or ovals, but pulled together for the eye by the interwoven linear tracings . . . bands . . . tendrils . . . ribbons . . . floral roundness, twining curves . . . ; and repeated, they build up seductive patterns and tracery winning to the eye. . . . The pleasure is sensuous; the values melodious and harmonic. . . . There is . . . a subtle balance of mathematical and free elements. The geometric, repetitive plan controls; yet the free contours are virile and the rhythm marked . . . In its ultimate . . . form . . . there is no beginning or end. . . . There is no point at which the eye comes to rest . . . [Cheney, 1945, pp. 373–375].

Exploring its rhythmicity, in Matisse's hands this abstract form became more openly sexualized *and* more delimited; hence, more energized. While he took away some of the

Henri Matisse: *Dance* (1910), oil 8' 5⅝" × 12' 9½" Moscow, Museum of Modern Western Art (ex Shchukin)

abstractness of the arabesque form, he related it directly to the form of woman's body; at the same time, he minimalized and thus abstracted the representation of her body.

Through these various checks and balances, intensifying here and reducing tension there, the contradictory sensations he experienced as emanating from woman's body became unified in a new equilibrium of feeling. He "created a new kind of beauty, at once female and modern—the paradoxical beauty of tension. Out of the trauma[tic impact] of woman's self-contradictory body he created modern traumatic beauty" (Kuspit, 1993, p. 28); in effect, he first "desexualized and idealized his mother into pure form ... [and was then] led ... to resexualize her" (Kuspit, p. 40) in the form of the arabesque.

But not only de- and resexualization was involved. Channeled aggressivization is also implicit in the physical act of his making cutouts of female figures. And perhaps it is redundant to point out that the sheer physical labor involved in the *making* of all art is replete with sexual and aggressive energies.

The power of art thus to tap, harness, and replenish (attune to) a full array of vital feelings, resonating in response, may be seen as analogous to the organizing strength of any ego to create its own intrapsychic equilibrium, and at the same time, strike a working balance with the outside world of reality.

To the extent that any art succeeds in seeming to flow anew—alive and free toward this goal—it may be taken as both enticement and ideal *model* for Everyman's ego–biological task to attempt likewise—if never as well.

6

IF I AM I . . . : ART AND EGO

If I am I because I am I,
and You are You because You are You,
then I am I, and You are You.
But
If I am I because You are You,
and You are You because I am I,
then I am not I and You are not You.
—Martin Buber

But, if I am not I, what then? May any I do?

It turned out to be the most memorable clinical experience of my first year of inhospital psychiatric training. Interviewing a young male schizophrenic patient, the conversation—if it may be called that—went something like this:

I: Please come in and sit down. I'd like to talk with you.
He: Please come in and sit down. I'd like to talk with you.
I: How long have you been in the hospital?
He: How long have you been in the hospital?
I: You're repeating everything I say. How come?
He: You're repeating everything I say. How come?

So *this* was "echolalia"! Noticing that he kept glancing at the dictaphone on my desk, I asked if he were interested in it. He repeated my words. I invited him to take a closer look at it if he liked. He repeated my words. I said he could have a better look if we swapped seats, and I got up and offered him my chair behind the desk, which he accepted, and I sat in his.

Then, to my astonishment, we had a normal conversation.

I repeated the "experiment" several times. Each time with the same results. Evidently there was much more involved in swapping places than just chairs. For him, position in life was literally everything. Was that what he was "saying"? Or was he showing me what it was like to feel he didn't have permission to have an ego of his own, or to use it to get himself "organized"? So he used me as an external prop— an auxiliary ego—to make up for what was lacking within? Me as part of an *external* spatial arrangement, a form, a shape, to bring some order to an *internal* life floating free of the gravitational force of a cohesive sense of self.

Let us return to the idea of form as an organizing shape, and consider art as another way of dealing with the dilemma, "If I am not I, what then?"

As part of the recent upsurge of interest in "Art Brut," raw art produced by persons outside the mainstream, unschooled "primitives," children, the autistic or insane, the story of Adolf Wölfli, a psychotic Swiss artist (1864–1930), is instructive (Morgenthaler, 1992).

After his mother died when he was about 8, he began his life as a hireling, working as a farm laborer for drunken, abusive employers and receiving little schooling. He was rejected in love at 18 and again, by a prostitute, at 24, but not without first contracting a venereal disease. He accosted young girls and finally a child of 3½, for which he was tried and imprisoned.

Working in the field with other prisoners—he was now

27—"a *shape* suddenly appeared to him which he said was the Holy Spirit, though at the same time he thought that it 'had to be my sweetheart'" (p. 7; emphasis added). Tormented as he was with uncontrolled violent and "lascivious" impulses, this visual hallucination was a self-created external *shape* embodying violent sexual desires loosely threaded within a defensive religious figuration.

We do not know what other intervening steps there were between this episode and ten years later, by which time he was bringing art to bear on the chaos of his life to create some degree of order for himself. We know only that by 31 he was hospitalized and remained there till his death at 66. He was paranoid, hypochondriacal, neurasthenic, and experienced visual and auditory hallucinations that often caused him to become violent—because of which he was in seclusion for twenty years.

Nor do we know how he discovered art as a means of "composing" himself to some extent. From age 37 to 55 he was endlessly drawing, painting, writing, composing music and poetry from morning till night. Even during his terminal illness of gastric cancer he drew a picture of himself on the operating table.

Wölfli always referred to this as play or a pastime. By whatever term, it was clear that it was profoundly necessary and serious. Though he still had periods of rage, arguing with his delusional tormentors, and responding with threats and violence to his auditory hallucinations, he would be calm as long as he had drawing material and no one interfered—as, for example, when it was suggested that he turn his zeal to something "useful" like basket-weaving. Not long after this he "declared that his taste for work had passed. . . . He had a serious attack of rage in his cell; he pulled out the sliding window, broke the thick glass and, white as a sheet, began to shout endlessly about his injuries until his rage suddenly broke into a violent attack of weeping" (p. 13).

Dr. Walter Morgenthaler was Wölfli's primary physician. It was he who saw to it that Wölfli was supplied with the art materials he preferred—mostly large sheets of newsprint and colored pencils. Morgenthaler noted that Wölfli could not tell even just before beginning to draw what he intended. The act of drawing, itself, would bring the thought. Once begun, he would carry it through, filling up all the spaces like a robot. Yet, the drawings show a distinctly personal style and a harmony of form and color rather than verisimilitude.

In the artwork Morgenthaler noted two contrasting phenomena. On the one hand a tremendous force and energy seems to strive for totality and freedom; on the other, a calm ordering and sense of objectivity works to integrate the overall composition but also leads to a freezing of the forms. The result lends a highly personal character to his work as Wölfli would give himself over totally to the "play" or "struggle" "between his natural instinct and his counterforce. . . . That is why his manner of creating and his works have for us such a character of necessity, or urgency. . . . He doesn't know the laws by which he works, but he obeys them unreservedly . . . [and] remains true to himself" (p. 90).

The later drawings are more conventionalized and personal, the forms stiffer and less realistic, but showing greater formal unity and decorativeness. "As Wölfli becomes calmer, as his instinctive force gives way . . . his works become more rigid, more empty. . . . But thanks to this regression of brute forces, an opposite movement, normative and regulatory, comes increasingly to the fore, bringing out the formal and essentially decorative aspect in his works" (p. 96).

Whether in drawing, poetry, or music, *rhythm* appears to be the most general ordering principle for Wölfli in the exercise of his innate talent. In his poetry, whatever formal unity and coherence there exists is imposed solely by rhythm; as sentence structure and even words progressively fall apart into syllables and letters, rhythm and sound—rather than meaning—determine how words are strung together. In his musical compositions his notational system has a decorative character. Again, rhythm is the essential element.

To the extent that the rhythmic forms in painting, music, or poetry succeeded in integrating conflicting forces within coherent boundaries they served to moderate from without what could not be contained within. Sometimes the content of the art would be openly sexual. More important, the very act of *making* art seemed to rhythmicize and thereby unify the powerful sexual and aggressive urges that otherwise exploded in behavior.

Art, in short, constituted an auxiliary ego. Each day through art he would rebuild an external "influencing machine" to replace and reinforce his faulty intrapsychic regulation. Where ego was—or should have been—art would come to be.

Since the ego is first and foremost a body ego—meaning that representations of the bodily self are at its core—the artwork externalizes the body ego. As such, it manifests the two phenomena that Morgenthaler noted: the tremendous force and energy reflecting the body's drives, as well as a regulatory principle. Rhythm, I suggest, bridges between both the inherent nature of drives and the rhythmic scanning by the thalamus of sensory input (?), and the elementary ordering of aesthetic form, relating Wölfli's art to body ego.

Before oversubscribing to art's lifesaving power to harness vital rhythm to aesthetic form and salvage a rudimentary self from total chaos, a cautionary note is indicated. Art—even in the presence of considerable talent—cannot always stabilize a disintegrating ego. Witness the tragic fate of Jackson Pollock.

His allover gestural works may well reflect psychological attempts "to take his insanity literally in hand before it took him entirely in its hands" (Kuspit, 1993, p. 127). But his rapid gesturalism—stylistic advance though it may have been—only bespeaks his ego's inability to regulate perceptual overstimulation as he strove to "lyricize his uncontainable aggression" (p. 130). As with Wölfli's art, rhythm stands out most. But the "composite of rhythms . . . are interrupted and broken—fragments . . . that trail off into inconsequence, like shooting stars" (p. 131). His art thus appears to have mirrored his life and prefigured its end.

In an open and healthy model of the organism there is an interplay of attunement and resonance between I and Thou. An ongoing "transitional process" may be thought of as outliving the transitional object, thus extending bridges from Winnicott's transitional object that provide a sense of coherence and meaning to existence. Underlying a dynamic reality there is a dialectic of fusion and reseparation. "The creativity of everyday life" is a way of talking about how early symbiotic modes of relating inner and outer do not atrophy and give way to "realistic" appreciation of separateness—any more than primary process gives way to the secondary process. Rather, they undergo continuing development and differentiation. At the same time, their interplay with well-delineated self and object representations contribute to the richness of life—including, especially, art and the creative process (Rose, 1963, 1964, 1966, 1971, 1973, 1978).

Such views open up new possibilities for growth and enhancement through the auspices of analytic therapy as well as a fuller understanding and appreciation of the psychological uses of art.

Regarding therapy, the views sketched above are now largely implicit in the current "postclassical" approach to analytic therapy (Jonghe, Rijnierse, and Janssen, 1991, 1992; Settlage, 1992), and the "intersubjective" nature of the analytic relationship (Usuelli, 1992; Ogden, 1994). Less a psychology of conflict than of developmental arrest in the early preoedipal period, treatment offers the opportunity for a "primary relationship." This consists of a reliving or rexperiencing of early modes of symbiotic relating and, more specifically, the trust of the early holding environment. Nonverbal support, *affective responsiveness*, and humaneness are preconditions for a later "classical" approach and intervention with curative interpretations (Kogan, 1993).

Regarding the psychological uses of art, there are several points of connection to our own discussion of emotional resonance and attunement in art: (1) the primary relationship, like the aesthetic experience, is characterized by a sense of nonverbal, intuitive feeling-understanding; (2) they both tap into a narcissistic quality that is an ever-present aspect of every relationship to some degree; (3) most pertinently, they both evoke memory traces of the early holding environment "which can subsequently be re-enacted in the quest for aesthetic experiences . . . [or] . . . anything that promises existential change . . ." (Treurniet, 1993, p. 876).

If it is the actual empathic support of a "postclassical" analytic therapy that can evoke memories of the primary relationship of the early holding environment, what is responsible for the same in the aesthetic experience? The dynamic interplay between the *apparent* attunement of aesthetic forms and one's responsive emotional resonances must provide the raw material for a preconscious illusion and fantasy: not only is one *not* alone, one is in a state of emotional accord with a responsive presence. Its quality of wordless harmony signals its primal origin: unconscious memory traces of an internalized early object.

The building of such affective personal meanings on the basis of an *illusion* of connectedness may well be part of the requisite response to all art. It is also much more than that. The sense of an emotionally responsive presence, illusional or not, is "witness" to an existential necessity: I *am* I.

The testimony of Aharon Appelfeld, the author and Holocaust survivor who spent his childhood years from 9 to 12 hiding in forests, traces some of the inner steps leading from prolonged existential crisis to self-preservation and, ultimately, the restoration of the "I" through art:

> Out of my great longing for my parents, I transported them to my hiding place, and I used to speak with them as if they were sitting by my side. Those conversations gave me a kind of joy and confidence, but above all, a feeling that I was not alone in the world. After the war other children told that they too had feelings like that in the forests [Appelfeld, 1994, p. 50].

Later: "Right after the war . . . there arose, inchoate and inarticulate, the first efforts at expression . . . [Later yet] the desire to keep silence and the desire to speak became deeper; and only artistic expression, which came years later, could attempt to bridge these two difficult imperatives" (p. 35). Artistic expression, when it did begin to come, began with children. They stood up on crates and sang, walked tightropes, juggled wooden balls, imitated animals and birds. Even in camps they drew pictures and wrote poems. "Artistic consciousness came later. There was a need not only for perspective, but also for some new orientation" (p. 38).

At first this meant the need for oblivion. Much later: "to bring it down to the human realm . . . to make the events speak through the individual . . . to rescue the suffering from . . . anonymity, and to restore the person's . . . name, to give . . . back his human form . . . (p. 39).

Finally:

> What . . . if not art . . . will take that great mass which everyone simply calls the "dreadful horror" and break it up into these tiny, precious particles? . . . Art cannot replace faith. Art lacks the power for that task, nor does it pretend to possess such power. Nonetheless, by its very nature, art constantly challenges the process by which the individual is reduced to anonymity [p. 23].

There is a long history to the important idea of the "restorative" function of art. About a century before John Dewey's (1934) *Art as Experience,* John Ruskin diagnosed the then current social ills as due to the ordinary worker being deprived by mechanization of the satisfaction that comes from making and doing with one's own hands. In the modern era, Walter Gropius of the Bauhaus pleaded for the centrality of artistic activity in any curriculum. The reason that artistic activity is universal is that it is a way of fostering developmental needs, most basically, for identity and mastery through personal expression.

Therefore, it should not be surprising that creditable results in addition to considerable satisfaction have resulted from encouraging artistic activity in various populations irrespective of innate talent or cultural background. Artist Henry Schaefer-Simmern, for example, taught art-making to mentally retarded, institutionalized individuals and to black and Hispanic children in a ghetto school. Poet Kenneth Koch taught poem-crafting to aged, ill, depressed, uneducated people in a nursing home (cf. Sarason, 1990).

Nor can there be any doubt that for working professional artists the making of art is a vehicle for growth and repair.

The work of a series of contemporary European artists, for example, has been shown by Kuspit (1993) to center around issues of personal trauma (Lassnig, Beuys), power (Kiefer), history (Richter), origins and identity (Bol-tanski), existential melancholy (Dokoupil).

As for the ways in which art may be used by any particular individual in the audience of art, they comprise a whole repertoire of possibilities according to the needs and circumstances of the moment and in line with that person's characteristic modes of responding and the nature of the early introjects. Is the individual's primary tendency to respond with confrontation, abreaction, identification, narcissistic withdrawal, mirroring? Is there the capacity, and is the timing ripe to foster reinternalization of basic psychological issues, provided they appear to be attuned to one's personality and are feelingly objectified in the artwork?

For the audience of art, participation in the aesthetic experience offers the opportunity for regression and/or progression, "escape" or expansion in a dynamically changing "living" balance. Such a wide range of possibilities, extending from the evocation of early mother-child affect states to a transforming emotional reintegration, marks the aesthetic experience as one of significant developmental *potential* as regards the differentiation of affects.

Early mothering in an optimal holding environment provides the basis for affects to begin to develop and differentiate along with self and object representations. Normally they continue to develop as part and parcel of important object relations and in all phases of psychosexual and psychosocial development. Life and clinical experience, now supplemented by developmental research, demonstrates that empathic feed-back of intimate relationships at any time in life can reactivate very early motivational processes and spur ongoing development (Emde, 1990). Further active recreation and mastery can take place in therapy as well as other intimate experiences. This may well include art.

This is not to suggest the existence of *any* royal road to empathy or emotional maturity. As with education, religion or, indeed, psychoanalysis, the yield from experiencing art probably depends on the use to which it is put— *perchance*, to grow. Just as art cannot always rescue and stabilize a disintegrating ego, experience and intuition tell us that, for artist as well as audience, art may simply succeed in "getting the better of forms," as from language "one has only learnt to get the better of words" (Eliot, 1943, p. 30). Or merely have the experience but miss the meaning (p. 39).

To the extent that art may play a potentiating role in emotional development, how may this be conceptualized? Art may reactivate early motivational processes by providing an *illusion* of responsiveness linked to internal objects. Basically this means that art may promote emotional development by advancing the biological function of early mothering together with the attunement and resonance inherent in this.

Spelling this out in greater detail, the establishment and organization of perceptual tensions in the artwork are so finely tuned that it offers an objective image of apparent attunement to the experience of human feelings. This structure fosters an illusion and fantasy of a welcoming, witnessing presence. Together, these factors provide the *objectification* needed for something to become real, and the "*permission*" to feel more than we—unsupported—might allow ourselves to feel. As a result, affects resonate and build up with modulated intensity and continue to differentiate.

Art might thus be considered a normative mode for stimulating and assimilating potentially dangerous degrees of affect—providing an opportunity for an ongoing extension of the limits of the bearable. Instead of a traumatic reexperiencing of affective storms, or a repression of affective signals with regressive resomatization and fragmentation, progressive integration can take place within the safe holding presence of the aesthetic structure. This would result in an interweaving of tension and release, greater tolerance for intensity and duration, and ongoing elaboration of nuanced feeling qualities into one felt emotion (Jacobson, 1971).

Let us flesh out this line of reasoning further in the light of both old and recent affect theory.

Affects tend to "amplify," lend urgency, and reinforce their own sources (Tomkins, 1980), a phenomenon analogous to what we have been terming *resonance*. Thus, one might reason as follows: (1) It is likely that the various emotional resonances to art—embedded reactions to shapes of stimuli, echoes of early interpersonal signaling, the interaction of knowledge and imagination within the spirit of the times—also become amplified in the course of the interplay between resonance and attunement. (2) It is reasonable that this amplification might reach the intensity of a "peak-affect state." Originally, this was a state that probably favored symbolization and was integrated with memories and early self and object representations (Kernberg, 1992). (3) Under the impact of emotional amplification, the aesthetic experience, itself, would come to represent a *current* edition of such a peak state. (4) As such, it would embody linkages to far-flung memories, symbolizations, internalized objects, and an early receptive sense of self.

For the artist, one may suppose that aesthetic form represents an externalization and a transformation of originally unmodified, emotional intensity into highly elaborated structures of interwoven tension and release. As in early motivation, emotion would be primary, aesthetic form the means of transforming it, and fantasy a concurrent or defensive way of dealing with it.

For the rest of us, the completed work of art may be used as an ambient context for creating an illusion of a witnessing presence to one's own emotions. This simulates or reinstates an *internalized* object, thus reclaiming access to an early *open* sense of self, now available to one's adult experience. This reopened early sense of self under the auspices of an enabling internalized structure—reaffirming while updating the "I am I" in the light of one's attained maturity—constitutes the nub of the developmental potential of art to facilitate ongoing emotional differentiation.

Since representations of the body are at the core of the ego, bodily tension and release accompany the making of art and may be evoked in experiencing it. When Osip Mandelstam, the greatest Russian poet of the modern era, would compose a poem, he would become very restless and need to keep moving. He would either pace the room or walk the streets to the point of exhaustion. If he stopped to rest he would lean for support with one hand and twirl his walking stick with the other.

In a chapter entitled "Moving Lips," his widow describes this motor restlessness as the first signal of a poem in process (Mandelstam, 1970, pp. 184–189). The second sign would be the moving of his lips for "since he works with his voice, a poet's lips are the tool of his trade" (p. 186). In one of his poems he writes that his lips can never be taken away from him and that they will still move when he is dead and buried.

In another one, about the flute player who "treads with his lips," she tells us that "he is also speaking about his own whispering lips and the painful process of converting into words the sounds ringing in his ears." "First . . . the lips move soundlessly, then they begin to whisper and at last the inner music resolves itself into units of meaning" (p. 187).

The meaning, she writes, has to do with recollection "of something that has never before been said, and the search for lost words is an attempt to remember what is still to be brought into being . . . till whatever has been forgotten suddenly flashes into the mind" (p. 187). Mandelstam insisted that the process of working on his poetry—starting with the initial "ringing in the ears," before the formation of words, already embodied content: "form and content are absolutely indivisible" (p. 187).

Recall Adolf Wölfli, the psychotic Swiss artist. For him, the very act of drawing would itself bring its own integration of personal style with harmony of form and color. As with Mandelstam's poetry, form and content do not *come* together; they *are* together *ab initio*.

Another point of similarity is the absolute *driven-ness* of their work. We have already described this as regards Wölfli. Of Mandelstam his widow writes:

> When the work is in progress, nothing can stop the inner voice, which . . . takes complete possession. . . . It is quite impossible for him to curb or silence himself by "stepping on the throat" of his own song. . . . His poetry would not leave him alone, bringing him nothing but misery and [in contrast to Wölfli] not allowing him to pursue his craft as a painter, the one thing that gave him pleasure [p. 188].

If we compare Wölfli's "poetry" with that of Mandelstam, the only unity and coherence that existed in that of Wölfli's was imparted to it by dint of its sense of rhythm. Sentences and words fell apart into syllables and letters that made patterns of sound without sense.

In Mandelstam's, on the other hand—and here we have

the crucial difference—not only is there sense, obviously, but the sense has to do with a feeling for *others*.

> The [poetic] urge ceases to be felt only when the poet's material begins to run out—that is, when his contact with the world at large is broken and he no longer hears his fellow men or lives with them. There can be no poetry without such contact, which is the source of the poet's sense of "rightness." The urge dies together with the poet, though the movement of his lips is recorded for all time in the verse he leaves behind [p. 188].

This is in the sharpest contrast with Wölfli, for whom art might be construed as an externalization of his body-ego. His art-as-body-ego, pretuned to the dynamic patterns of tension and release of his own vital rhythms and those sensed in the external world, could then serve as a template or temporary scaffold re-assembled each day to provide a rudimentary sense of self. The physical act of making art, and the artwork itself, helped relate him to himself in a world of his own making.

The artwork, itself, however, does not reach out; it assimilates without accommodating. His drawing, *Mental Asylum Band-hain*, is "a maze of monumental weight with no way in or out. Yet, [its] delicate . . . architecture of a fantastic, cellular kind . . . has an organic quality. It pervades the entire structure, like body heat . . . [It] acknowledge[s] the outer world only by incorporating it into a map of his interior . . . [It] shows the inmate as asylum, asylum as inmate (Ratcliff, 1988, p. 21).

This would seem to place Wölfli's art, masterful though it may be, outside one definition of art that holds that even though an artist can be mad, madness cannot be art (Ratcliff, 1988). The argument is that art is an exercise in rhetoric within a social contract. However vigorously it attempts

Wölfli: *The Mental Asylum Band-hain* (1910). Adolf Wölfi Foundation Museum of Fine Arts, Berne.

to persuade and overcome the resistance of an audience, so long as it serves to *bridge* between the I and thou it cannot be held to be mad even though the artist may periodically disappear into madness (Gauguin, Blake, Van Gogh). The artist may even play at madness to temporarily derange the senses and defamiliarize the ordinary to challenge an audience and awaken it from its perceptual somnambulism. If the ideals of rational selfhood remain implicit, and a professional heritage and a social contract are acknowledged, extending one's "private mythology" to make oneself understood to others fulfills the aim of art: to make separateness more workable, otherness less alien, the world more expansive, the self more whole.

Thus, Mandelstam, though he experienced auditory hallucinations at times when subjected to brutal and prolonged harassment, nevertheless wrote poetry that was an expression of a Self in a real relation *to* an Other rather than each fused *with* Other. While intimately related to the world personally and through his poetry, I and Thou existed in a state of mutual enhancement *and* separateness.

Referring back to Buber's quotation at the head of this chapter, art would speak for this more open interplay between Inner and Outer while preserving the autonomy of boundaries:

> I would be I because I am I as well as because You are You. You would be You because You are You as well as because I am I. We would keep being both more and less than what we had supposed, as each remained one's self, surely.
> But not only.

Mandlestam appears to have been an admirable human being as well as a great artist, combining empathy in life with intuition in art. What an exception (!) to the histories of so many great artists whose generosity toward others could be exceeded only by their cruelty, or their self sacrifice by self-indulgence. In their own medium, like Picasso, transforming pieces of junk into works of "living" art, while treating people like things, and all the while demanding their absolute, one-sided devotion.

An example of this well-known genre, too extreme even for his own operatic stage, is the life of the composer Verdi, who knew how to be humane and often chose to be brutal. Item (Phillips-Matz, 1993): in furious response to his father's disapproval for having abandoned two illegitimate children, he obtained a legal separation from his parents to whom he was financially in debt, and kicked them out of their house which sat on land he owned. (His mother died a few weeks after the dispossession).

How can one describe in intrapsychic terms, let alone explain, these vast differences in character coexisting with creative giftedness? May it lie along the lines of the dialectic previously alluded to: the two kinds of persisting intrapsychic symbiotic self-representations—the attached mode, more or less lost in its union with the maternal representation; and the separateness mode, expanded to include the maternal representation? (Blatt and Blass, 1990).

Would this not have to include a further interplay with clearly delineated self and object representations (cf. Chapter 4, pp. 71–72)? To further complicate matters, one would have to assume that all three modes of representation coexist in chains of parallel but unequal development, linked to symbolizations, affective memories and an evolving sense of coherent identity. Finally, may an especially heightened propensity for symbiotic modes of representation be related to giftedness for creative artistic illusions as well as "unconventionalities" of character and identity?

These questions touch on the fundamental theoretical

issue of the relationship between (ego) internalization and sublimation. While they are admittedly not easy to distinguish (Loewald, 1988), it may be useful to assay some similarities and differences.

We begin by suggesting that sublimation is to the external world much as internalization is to the ego. Both effect transformations in the intermediate area where internal and external reality interpenetrate. These transformations represent a process of change from a lower to a higher level of organization in terms of range and degree of differentiation, in the course of which the force of passions is channeled and modulated rather than repressed or overcome. Internalization is more than incorporation or identification; sublimation is more than a defense. Internalization transforms the *ego* with new structuralization. Sublimation enriches the experience of *reality* with new meaning and sensuousness (Rose, 1980, 1987, 1990).

Internalization and sublimation may both be thought of as adaptations to loss. They compensate for loss by perpetuating a *continuity of form* in the internal or external world respectively. Just as the "right" doses of object loss at the appropriate stages fosters (*auto*plastic) internalization, the often traumatic loss of early relationships can also foster attempts at mastery through (*allo*plastic) symbolic repetitions, and reexperiencings. This spans a spectrum of pathology; it also includes the *possibility* of sublimation (Rose, 1987).

Before going into this let us clarify what is meant by a "continuity of form" that is common to both internalization and sublimation.

Abstraction, I suggest, is the means by which a continuity of form is achieved. Abstraction needs to be distinguished from repression and denial. The latter defend against conflict and anxiety by deleting from awareness internal and external events respectively; they thereby constrict the scope of reality. Abstraction, on the other hand, is essentially conflict-free and not necessarily connected with anxiety. While it passes over some elements of reality it does so in order to bring out new configurations at a higher (more integrated) plane. Thus, at a cultural level, by virtue of abstraction, each of the great symbolic forms—art, language, science—pass over certain parts of immediate factuality and constitute reality from several unique directions (Cassirer 1923).

In (ego) internalization, the *quality* of self-object relationships is abstracted, imparting the same quality to intrapsychic interactions. In sublimation, too, the quality of relationships is abstracted but self and objects may or may not be wholly differentiated to begin with, their interactions perhaps insufficiently internalized, or not well integrated with realistically delineated, nonsymbiotic self and object representations. In other words, significant relationships and their intrapsychic representations are likely to carry a strong symbiotic character.

This relates back to the question of loss. It has often been remarked that the creative person appears to be loss-sensitive and separation-prone (Rose, 1987, pp. 117–134). Perhaps because of a greater constitutional sensitivity to inner and outer sensuous forms (Greenacre, 1957), the process of individuation itself might be experienced as fraught with loss. For example, irrespective of actual loss as by personal disability or the death or abandonment by loved ones, the inadvertent but inevitable lapses of empathy on the part of even the most ideally attuned caretaker (or therapist) may be experienced as mismatching and a sense of alienation. Thus, a predominance of symbiotic over nonsymbiotic intrapsychic representations might well represent an inner defense against loss, while increasing its actual likelihood, and stimulating repeated efforts to overcome it through one's own creative work.

Assuming that the symbiotic quality of intrapsychic representations might be related to loss-sensitivity and sublimation allows the following to fall into place:

1. Being doubly-rooted in self and world makes them especially prone to be displaced and projected back to the external world.

2. This sensitizes one to a more general congruence of sentient shapes of tension and release between self and world.

3. As previously discussed, this entails an interplay of apparent attunement and responsive affective resonances. This tends to self-amplify toward peak-affect states and to be accompanied by the illusion and/or fantasy of a responsive presence, thus compensating for the experience of loss.

Once embarked on projection and reintrojection back and forth between self and world, congruent sentient shapes and their associated affective memories and symbolizations are the raw material for the creation of aesthetic forms. With the help of abstraction, they become objectified, elaborated and sharpened until sublimation succeeds in transcending the personal and concentrating the dynamic of aesthetic tension/release with economic clarity. Thus: the jazz improvisationist Miles Davis: "I listen for what I can leave out." Mandelstam, composing a poem, would have to "drive out" the "foreign bodies" with just the right word (Mandelstam, 1970, p. 71). As noted in the case of Mozart, music might evolve from a personal struggle with intrapsychic separateness and (re)attachment to achieve a higher level of organization where passionate but abstract forces contend and collaborate in an interplay of sameness with difference, union and separation, solo and tutti, presence and absence, sound and silence.

Since every propensity carries with it its own vulnerability, the combination of relatively more symbiotic types of representation plus an overdeveloped ability to abstract in the service of creative forms may be responsible in part for blunting or even derailing the capacity for human relationships. It is as though some artists refine the capacity for empathy in the abstract (Greenacre's [1957] "collective alternates") at the price of narcissistic personal relations. "Living" aesthetic forms of responsive creative illusion may supersede actual persons in living form.

To expand on this less moralistically, instead of building on a sound sense of self growing out of the internalization and integration of symbiotic with nonsymbiotic, realistic intrapsychic representations, a sublimation may substitute an *external* integration. This offers an alternative route of development via symbolic repetition and reexperiencing that by-passes or compromises the growth of full object relationships. Art and imposture, for example, may become related (Greenacre, 1958), presenting the paradox of authentic art together with inauthentic author.

One type of corresponding tilt in the opposite direction is the frequent concurrence of a highly developed capacity for critical and self-critical thought along with an incapacity to produce any modestly original work of sublimation.

Thus it appears that, while internalization and sublimation correspond in a number of respects, this does not imply a reciprocal, two-way relationship between them. No amount of ego structuralization via internalization endows an individual with the creative imagination that becomes actualized—realized—in sublimation. Nor is a creative artist immune to the human propensity to be as emotionally immature as the less endowed. A fortunate equilibrium between internalization and sublimation remains an ideal of health and creative living.

For the gifted and ungifted alike, as for artist and audience, it may be true, as some philosophers hold, that intuitive "knowledge" was the ultimate ground of real knowledge. Intuition refers to an illusion of knowing something external from within. It has a somewhat more cognitive connotation than the illusion of emotional responsiveness based on attunement and resonance. Both share a sensitivity to the felt patterns among sentient forms and an immediate and direct awareness of the underlying congruence among them. Perhaps they both derive from an illusion of symbiotic connectedness: intuition arising from the separateness mode of representation and emotional responsiveness from the attachment type.

The two-edged quality of propensity joined to its own vulnerability is well illustrated in the notion of illusion. Greek myth escalated the combination into the dramatic play of Philoctetes' magically unerring bow inseparably linked to his also having an incurably suppurating Achilles heel. Psychoanalysis prioritized the negative aspects of illusion in large measure, though not exclusively by any means (e.g., Freud's [1908] "Creative Writers and Daydreaming"), scorning it as deception and escape from reality.

Accordingly, the transformative power of illusion to civilize (Cassirer, 1923) has been largely overlooked. This was an understandable biproduct of the logical positivism of Freud's time that aspired to logically clarify thought processes and decontaminate them from emotion. In the excitement of discovering and exploring the "basement" foundation of the human edifice, it was easy to lose sight of the value of the view afforded from the upper stories.

Thanks largely to the *oeuvre* of Winnicott, we are now more aware that the ontological (existential) source of the self is itself founded on a floating base of illusion. In the spirit of modernism we struggle with the realization that nothing is dependable except change—with its restless search for the forms of reality within the rhythms of perpetual disintegration and renewal, ambiguity and contradiction (Berman, 1982). Instead of being able to take cover in a standing forest of manmade concepts—often somewhat arbitrary and reflecting merely the current consensus—the dilemma and challenge of our present perspective is to work and love fairly peaceably in the absence of certainty and in the silence of indeterminacy.

Trying to live imaginatively and creatively in the "real" world without undue despair or presumption may well entail living with illusions, knowing they are illusions, but valuing them for their function, indeed, their necessity, perhaps even creating new ones.

The illusion of a responsive presence in the form of art confirms that I am I and, like art, itself, perhaps perfectible in the confident expectation of a future which one knows is also an illusion, while true as far as it goes because in the service of life.

The necessity for illusion extends further. The poet writes:

Desire is our door into the world. We see shapes there and want them and we go after them into the world. But desire is our door out again also when the shapes we saw leave our desires unsatisfied. What could we ever have wanted? More than a door to enter, the world offers us a prospect to peer into whose shapes suggest a reality which they, themselves, are not. . . . Reality is shapeless and disparate [Bronk, 1985, p. 51].

What are these "shapes" the poet insistently refers to—

shapes seen through the doorway of desire leading into the world? They are shapes of early feeling, sought in the outside world, to be recaptured in the present, if only through the beneficence of the controlled illusion that is art: an objective realization that witnesses the ongoing interplay between self and other, luring life on beyond itself in the illusion of a future attuned to transformations at higher levels of the same resonating responsiveness that existed in the beginning.

REFERENCES

Allegro, J. (1977), *Lost Gods*. London.

Anderson, E., Ed. (1938), *The Letters of Mozart and His Family*, 3rd ed. New York: W. W. Norton, 1966.

Appelfeld, A. (1994), *Beyond Despair*. New York: Fromm International.

Arnheim, R. (1949), The Gestalt theory of expression. *Psychiatry Rev.*, 56:156–171.

—— (1954), *Art and Visual Perception: A Psychology of the Creative Eye*. Berkeley & Los Angeles: University of California Press.

—— (1966), *Toward a Psychology of Art*. Berkeley & Los Angeles: University of California Press.

Beckett, S. (1951), Malone Dies. In: *Three Novels by Samuel Beckett*. New York: Grove Press, 1965.

Berman, M. (1982), *All That Is Solid Melts Into Air*. New York: Simon & Schuster.

Blass, R. B., & Blatt, S. J. Attachment and separateness in the experience of symbiotic relatedness. Typescript.

Blatt, S. J., & Blass, R. B. (1990), Attachment and separateness. A dialectic model of the products and processes of development throughout the life cycle. *Psychoanalytic Study of the Child*, 45:107–127.

—— Shichman, S. (1983), Two primary configurations of psychopathology. *Psychoanal. & Contemp. Thought*, 6:187–254.

Blom, E., Ed. (1954), *Grove's Dictionary of Music and Musicians*, Vol. 5, 5th ed. New York: Macmillan, pp. 923–982.

Brenman-Gibson, M. (1981), *Clifford Odets. American Playwright*. New York: Atheneum.

Brenner, C. (1974), On the nature and development of affects: A unified theory. *Psychoanal. Quart.*, 44:532–556.

Brettell, R., Cachin, F., Freches-Thory, C., & Stuckey, C. F. (1988), *The Art of Paul Gauguin*. Washington, DC: National Gallery of Art.

Brierley, M. (1937), Affects in theory and practice. *Internat. J. Psycho-Anal.*, 18:256–268.

Bronk, W. (1985), *Vectors and Smoothable Curves*. San Francisco: North Point Press.

Buber, M. (1963), Man and his image-work, tr. M. Friedman. *Portfolio*, 7:88–99.

Cahill, L., Prins, B., Weber, M., & McGaugh, J. L. (1994), Beta Adrenergic activation and memory for emotional events. *Nature*, 371:702–704, #6499.

Cassirer, E. (1923), *The Philosophy of Symbolic Forms*, Vol. 1. New Haven, CT: Yale University Press, 1953.

Chekhov, A. (1889), The Swan Song. In: *Plays by Anton Tchekoff*, tr. M. Fell. New York: Scribner's, 1916, pp. 223–233.

Cheney, S. (1945), *World History of Art*. New York: Viking.

Clynes, M., & Nettheim, N. (1982), The living quality of music. In: *Music, Mind, and Brain. The Neuropsychology of Music*. New York & London: Plenum, pp. 47–82.

Cone, E. T., Ed. (1979), *Roger Sessions on Music*. Princeton, NJ: Princeton University Press.

Darwin, C. (1872), *The Expression of Emotions in Man and Animals*. Chicago: University of Chicago Press, 1965.

Davies, P. J. (1993), Mozart's health, illnesses, and death. In: *The Pleasures and Perils of Genius: Mostly Mozart*. Madison, CT.: International Universities Press, pp. 97–107.

Dewey, J. (1934), *Art as Experience*. New York: Minton, Balch.

Dissanayake, E. (1992), *Homo Aestheticus*. New York: Free Press.

Eliot, T. S. (1943), *Four Quartets*. New York: Harcourt Brace Jovanovich, 1971.

—— (1957), The Music of Poetry. In: *On Poets and Poetry*. New York: Farrar, Straus & Cudahy.

Emde, R. N. (1983), The prerepresentational self and its affective core. In: *The Psychoanalytic Study of the Child*, 38:165–192. New Haven, CT: Yale University Press.

—— (1990), Mobilizing fundamental modes of development: Empathic availability and therapeutic action. *J. Amer. Psychoanal. Assn.*, 38:881–913.

Epstein, D. (1993), On affect in musical motion. In: *Psychoanalytic Explorations in Music. Second Series*, ed. S. Feder, R. L. Karmel, & G. H. Pollock. Madison, CT: International Universities Press, pp. 91–123.

—— (1995), *Shaping Time: Music, The Brain, and Performance*. New York: Schirmer Books/Macmillan.

Erikson, E. (1954), The dream specimen of psychoanalysis. *J. Amer. Psychoanal. Assn.*, 2:5–56.

Esman, A. H. (1994), Pollock's "psychoanalytic" drawings and the search for the "innner life." *Psychoanal. & Contemp. Thought*, 17:129–135.

Feder, L. (1980), *Madness in Literature*. Princeton, NJ: Princeton University Press.

Feder, S. (1990), The nostalgia of Charles Ives: An essay in affects and music. In: *Psychoanalytic Explorations in Music*, ed. S. Feder, R. L. Karmel, & G. H. Pollock. Madison, CT: International University Press, pp. 233–266.

—— (1993a), "Promissory notes": Method in music and applied psychoanalysis. In: *Psychoanalytic Explorations in Music, Second Series*, ed. S. Feder, R. L. Karmel, & G. H. Pollock. Madison, CT: International Universities Press, pp. 3–19.

—— (1993b), Mozart in D Minor. In: *The Pleasures and Perils of Genius: Mostly Mozart*, ed. P. Ostwald & L. S. Zegans. Madison, CT: International Universities Press, pp. 117–131.

Felman, S., & Laub, D. (1992), *Testimony*. New York & London: Routledge.

Findlay, A. (1948), *A Hundred Years of Chemistry*, 2nd ed. London: Duckworth.

Fuller, P. (1980), *Art and Psychoanalysis*. London: Writers & Readers Publishing Cooperative.

Freud, S. (1895), Project for a Scientific Psychology. *Standard Edition*, 1. London: Hogarth Press, 1966.

—— (1900), The Interpretation of Dreams. *Standard Edition*, 4 & 5. London: Hogarth Press, 1953.

—— (1908), Creative writers and day-dreaming. *Standard Edition*, 9:143–153. London: Hogarth Press, 1959.

—— (1914), The Moses of Michelangelo. *Standard Edition*, 13:211–238. London: Hogarth Press, 1955.

—— (1915), Instincts and their vicissitudes. *Standard Edition*, 14:117–140. London: Hogarth Press, 1957.

—— (1923), The ego and the id. *Standard Edition*, 19:12–66. London: Hogarth Press, 1961.

—— (1924), The economic problem of masochism. *Standard Edition*, 19:157–170. London: Hogarth Press, 1961.

—— (1925), Negation. *Standard Edition*, 19:235–239. London: Hogarth Press, 1961.

—— (1926), Inhibitions, symptoms and anxiety. *Standard Edition*, 20:87–172. London: Hogarth Press, 1959.

Gauguin, P. (1919), *Noa Noa. The Tahitian Journal*. New York: Dover Publications, 1985.

—— (1921), *Paul Gauguin's Intimate Journals*. tr. Van Wyck Brooks. New York & London: Liveright, 1949.

—— (1974), *Writings of a Savage*, ed. D. Guerin. New York: Viking Press, 1977.

Gay, V. P. (1992), *Freud on Sublimation: Reconsiderations*. SUNY Series in Religious Studies. Albany: State University of New York Press.

Gedo, J. (1994), The inner world of Paul Gauguin. *The Annual of Psychoanalysis*, 22:61–109.

Gibson, J. J. (1979), *The Ecological Approach to Visual Perception*. Boston: Houghton Mifflin.

Gilot, F., & Lake, C. (1964), *Life with Picasso*. New York: McGraw-Hill, pp. 276–277.

Glauber, I. P. (1937), The rebirth motif in homosexuality and its teleological significance. *Internat. J. Psycho-Anal.*, 37:416–421.

Goldsmith, G. (1992), Freud's aesthetic response to Michelangelo's Moses. *Annual of Psychoanalysis*, 20:245–269. Hillside, NJ: Analytic Press.

Goldwater, R. (1983), *Gauguin*. New York: Abrams.

Green, A. (1986), *On Private Madness*. Madison, CT: International Universities Press.

Greenacre, P. (1957), The childhood of the artist. *The Psychoanalytic Study of the Child*, 12:47–72. New York: International Universities Press.

—— (1958), The relation of the impostor to the artist. *The Psychoanalytic Study of the Child*, 13:521–540. New York: International Universities Press.

Hartmann, H. (1956), Notes on the reality principle. In: *Essays on Ego Psychology*. New York: International Universities Press, 1964, pp. 241–267.

Hegel, F. (1807), *The Phenomenology of Spirit*, tr. A. V. Miller. Oxford: Oxford University Press, 1977.

Isaacs, S. (1943), The nature and function of fantasy. In: *Developments in Psychoanalysis*, ed. M. Klein, P. Heimonn, S. Isaacs, & J. Riviere. London: Hogarth Press, 1952. pp. 57–121.

Jacobson, E. (1971), *Depression*. New York: International Universities Press.

Jakobson, R., & Waugh, L. (1979), *The Sound Shape of Language*. Bloomington: Indiana University Press.

Jonghe, F., Rijnierse, P., & Janssen, R. (1991), Aspects of the analytic relationship. *Internat. J. Psycho-Anal.*, 72:693–707.

—— —— —— (1992), The role of support in psychoanalysis. *J. Amer. Psychoanal. Assn.*, 40:475–499.

Kapferer, B. (1983), *A Celebration of Demons: Exorcism and the Aesthetics of Healing in Sri Lanka*. Bloomington: Indiana University Press.

Kernberg, O. F. (1992), *Aggression in Personality Disorders and Perversions. New Perspectives on Drive Theory*. New Haven & London: Yale University Press.

—— (1993), The Erotic Element in Mass Psychology and in Art. Paper read at Westchester Psychoanalytic Society, February 1.

Kierkegaard, S. (1843), *Either/Or*, Vol. 1, tr. D. F. Swenson & L. M. Swenson. Garden City, NY: Anchor/Doubleday, 1959.

Kinsey, A. C., Pomeroy, W. B., & Martin, C. E. (1948), *Sexual Behavior in the Human Male*. Philadelphia & London: W. B. Saunders.

Kirshner, L. A. (1991), The concept of the self. *J. Amer. Psychoanal. Assn.*, 39:157–182.

—— (1993), Concepts of reality and psychic reality in psychoanalysis as illustrated by the disagreement between Freud and Ferenczi. *Internat. J. Psycho-Anal.*, 74:219–230.

Klein, M. (1957), Envy and gratitude. In: *The Writings of Melanie Klein*, Vol. 3, ed. R. Money-Kyrle. London: Hogarth Press, 1984, pp. 176–235.

Koestler, A. (1964), *The Act of Creation*. New York: Macmillan.

Kogan, I. (1993), Curative factors in the psychoanalyses of Holocaust survivors' offspring before and during the Gulf War. *Internat. J. Psycho-Anal.*, 74:803–914.

Kris, E. (1952), *Psychoanalytic Explorations in Art*. New York: International Universities Press.

Kubie, L. S. (1974), The drive to become both sexes. *Psychoanal. Quart.*, 43:349–426.

Kuspit, D. (1993), *Signs of Psyche in Modern and Postmodern Art*. Cambridge, U.K.: Cambridge University Press.

Langer, S. (1953), *Feeling and Form*. New York: Scribner's.

—— (1967), *Mind: An Essay on Human Feeling*. Baltimore: Johns Hopkins University Press.

Lao Tze (c. 600 B.C.), *Tao Te Ching*, tr. Ch'u Ta Kao. London: Buddhist Society, 1937.

LeDoux, J., Romanski, L., & Xagoraris, A. (1989), Indelibility of subcortical emotional memories. *J. Cog. Neurosci.*, 1:238–243.

Liebert, R. (1983), *Michelangelo*. New Haven, CT: Yale University Press.

Loewald, H. (1988), *Sublimation*. New Haven, CT: Yale University Press.

Lorand, S. (1934), A note on the psychology of the inventor. *Psychoanal. Quart.*, 3:30–41.

Macalpine, I., & Hunter, R. A. (1953), The Schreber case. *Psychoanal. Quart.*, 22:328–371.

Mandelstam, N. (1970), *Hope Against Hope*. New York: Atheneum.

Milner, M. (1957), *On Not Being Able to Paint*. New York: International Universities Press.

—— (1973), Some notes on psychoanalytic ideas about mysticism. In: *The Suppressed Madness of Sane Men*. London & New York: Tavistock Publications, 1987.

Morgenthaler, W. (1992), *Madness and Art. The Life and Works of Adolf Wölfli*, Vol. 3, tr. by A. H. Esman with E. Spoerri. Texts and Contexts, Lincoln: University of Nebraska Press.

Motherwell, R. (1991), Interview for Public Television Series "American Masters," first broadcast August 26, 1991.

Neubauer, J. (1986), *The Emancipation of Music from Language*. New Haven, CT: Yale University Press.

Niederland, W. (1959), Schreber, father and son. *Psychoanal. Quart.*, 28:151–169.

O'Donohue, D. (1993), Absence and its contribution to the unfolding drama of the first movements of Mozart's D-Minor and C-Minor piano concertos. Typescript.

Ogden, T. H. (1994), The analytic third: Working with intersubjective clinical facts. *Internat. J. Psycho-Anal.*, 75:3–19.

O'Malley, J. W. (1979), *Praise and Blame in Renaissance Rome: Rhetoric, Doctrine, and Reform in Sacred Orators of the Papal Court, c. 1450–1521*. Durham, NC: Duke University Press.

Oremland, J. D. (1985), Michelangelo's *Ignudi*, hermaphrodism, and creativity. *The Psychoanalytic Study of the Child*, 40:399–433. New Haven, CT: Yale University Press.

Orland, F. (1971), Factors in autofellatio formation. *Internat. J. Psycho-Anal.*, 52:289–296.

Panel (1980), New knowledge about the infant from current research: Implications for psychoanalysis. L. Sander, reporter. *J. Amer. Psychoanal. Assn.*, 28:181–198.

Pater, W. (1873), The Renaissance. "The School of Georgione." In: *MacGill's Quotations in Context.* New York: Harper, 1973.

Peyre, H. (1974), *What Is Symbolism?* tr. E. Parker. Tuscaloosa: University of Alabama Press, 1980.

Philips-Matz, M. J. (1993), *Verdi: A Biography.* New York: Oxford University Press.

Rapaport, D. (1957), The theory of ego autonomy. In: *Collected Papers.* New York: Basic Books, 1967.

Ratcliff, C. (1988), Adolf Wölfli. In: *The Other Side of the Moon. The World of Adolf Wölfli.* Philadelphia: Goldie Paley Gallery, Moore College of Art, pp. 17–30.

Reiser, M. (1984), *Mind, Brain, Body.* New York: Basic Books.

—— (1990), *Meaning in Mind and Brain. What Dream Imagery Reveals.* New Haven, CT: Yale University Press, 1994.

Rice, E. (1990), *Freud and Moses.* Albany: State University of New York Press.

Richards, A. K., & Richards, A. D., Eds. (1994), *The Spectrum of Psychoanalysis.* Madison, CT: International Universities Press.

Riviere, J. (1936), On the genesis of psychical conflict in earliest infancy. *Internat. J. Psycho-Anal.*, 17:395–422.

Rose, G. J. (1961), Pregenital aspects of pregnancy fantasies. *Internat. J. Psycho-Anal.*, 42:544–549.

—— (1962), Unconscious birth fantasies in the ninth month of treatment. *J. Amer. Psychoanal. Assn.*, 10:677–688.

—— (1963), Body ego and creative imagination. *J. Amer. Psychoanal. Assn.*, 11:775–789.

—— (1964), Creative imagination in terms of ego "core" and boundaries. *Internat. J. Psycho-Anal.*, 45:75–84.

—— (1966), Body ego and reality. *Internat. J. Psycho-Anal.*, 47:502–509.

—— (1969), Transference birth fantasies and narcissism. *J. Amer. Psycho-Anal. Assn.*, 17:1015–1029.

—— (1971), Narcissistic fusion states and creativity. In: *The Unconscious Today,* ed. M. Kanzer. New York: International Universities Press, pp. 495–505.

—— (1972), Bleeding ulcer: A "bioversary" case study. *Internat. J. Psycho-Anal. Psychother.*, 1:68–77.

—— (1973), On the shores of self: Samuel Beckett's "Molloy"—Irredentism and the creative impulse. *Psychoanal. Rev.*, 60:587–604.

——— (1978), The creativity of everyday life. In: *Between Reality and Fantasy. Transitional Objects and Phenomena*, ed. S. Grolnick & L. Barkin. New York: Jason Aronson, pp. 345–362.

——— (1980), *The Power of Form. A Psychoanalytic Approach to Aesthetic Form*, rev. ed. New York: International Universities Press, 1992.

——— (1987), *Trauma and Mastery in Life and Art*. New Haven, CT: Yale University Press.

——— (1990), From ego-defense to reality enhancement: Updating the analytic perspective on art. *Amer. Imago*, 47:69–79.

——— (1991), Abstract art and emotion: Expressive form and the sense of wholeness. *J. Amer. Psychoanal. Assn.*, 39:131–156.

——— (1992), *The Power of Form: A Psychoanalytic Approach to Aesthetic Form*, Expanded Edition. Madison, CT: International Universities Press.

——— (1993), On form and feeling in music. In: *Psychoanalytic Explorations in Music. Second Series*, ed. S. Feder, R. L. Karmel, & G. H. Pollock. Madison, CT: International Universities Press, pp. 63–81.

Rowley, G. (1947), *Principles of Chinese Painting*. Princeton, NJ: Princeton University Press.

Sandler, J. (1987), The role of affects in psychoanalytic theory. In: *From Safety to Superego*. New York: Guilford Press, pp. 285–297.

Sarason, S. B. (1990), *The Challenge of Art to Psychology*. New Haven, CT: Yale University Press.

Saslow, J. M. (1986), *Ganymede in the Renaissance. Homosexuality in Art and Society*. New Haven & London: Yale University Press.

Sass, L. A. (1992), *Madness and Modernism. Insanity in the Light of Modern Art, Literature, and Thought*. New York: Basic Books.

Schreber, D. P. (1903), *Memoirs of My Nervous Illness*, tr. I. Macalpine & R. A. Hunter. Cambridge, MA: Harvard University Press, 1955.

Settlage, C. F. (1992), Psychoanalytic observations on adult development in life and in the therapeutic relationship. *Psychoanal. & Contemp. Thought*, 15:349–374.

Stein, R. (1991), *Psychoanalytic Theories of Affect*. New York: Praeger.

Stern, D. (1985), *The Interpersonal World of the Infant: A View from Psychoanalysis and Developmental Psychology*. New York: Basic Books.

Spitz, E. H. (1989), Psychoanalysis and the legacies of antiquity. In: *Sigmund Freud and Art: His Personal Collection of Antiquities*, ed. L. Gamwell & R. Wells. Binghamton, NY: State University of New York, pp. 153–177.

——— (1991), *Image and Insight: Essays in Psychoanalysis*. New York: Columbia University Press.

Tardieu, E. (1895), La peinture et les peintres, M. Paul Gauguin. *Echo de Paris*, May 13.

Tolstoy, L. N. (1951). *Collected Works*, Vol. 30. Moscow.

Tomkins, S. S. (1962–1963), *Affect, Imagery, Consciousness*, 2 vols. New York: Springer.

—— (1980), Affect as amplification: Some modification in theory. In: *Emotions: Theory, Research and Experience*, ed. R. Plutchik & H. Kellerman. New York: Academic Press, pp. 141–164.

—— (1981), The quest for primary motives: Biography and autobiography of an idea. *J. Personal. & Soc. Psychol.*, 41:306–329.

Treurniet, N. (1993), What is psychoanalysis now? *Internat. J. Psycho-Anal.*, 74:873–891.

Tschekoff, A. (1889), *The Swan Song*, tr. M. Fell. New York: Scribner's, pp. 223–233.

Usuelli, A. K. (1992), The significance of illusion in the work of Freud and Winnicott: A controversial issue. *Internat. Rev. Psycho-Anal.*, 19:179–187.

Vygotsky, L. S. (1971), *The Psychology of Art*. Cambridge, MA: M.I.T. Press.

Wilson, A., & Malatesta, C. (1989), Affect and the compulsion to repeat: Freud's repetition compulsion revisited. *Psychoanal. & Contemp. Thought*, 12:265–312.

Winnicott, D. W. (1953), Transitional objects and "phenomena." *Internat. J. Psycho-Anal.*, 34:89–97.

—— (1960), The theory of the parent-infant relationship. In: *The Maturational Processes and the Facilitating Environment*, New York: International Universities Press, pp. 37–55.

Wittgenstein, L. (1953), *Philosophical Investigations*. Tuscaloosa: University of Alabama Press.

Woods, G. (1987), *Articulate Flesh*. New Haven, CT: Yale University Press.

Yerushalmi, Y. H. (1991), *Freud's Moses*. New Haven, CT: Yale University Press.

Zuckerkandl, V. (1956), *Sound and Symbol*. Princeton, NJ: Princeton University Press, 1973.

—— (1973), *Man the Musician. Sound and Symbol*, Vol. 2. Princeton, NJ: Princeton University Press.

NAME INDEX

SUBJECT INDEX

141